THE GENESIS OF SHAKESPEARE'S
MERCHANT OF VENICE

Christopher Spencer

THE GENESIS OF SHAKESPEARE'S
MERCHANT OF VENICE

Christopher Spencer

Studies in British Literature
Volume 3

The Edwin Mellen Press
Lewiston/Queenston
Lampeter

Library of Congress Cataloging-in-Publication Data

Spencer, Christopher.
    The genesis of Shakespeare's Merchant of Venice / Christopher
Spencer.
       p. cm. -- (Studies in British Literature ; v. 3)
    Bibliography: p.
    Includes index.
    ISBN 0-88946-930-X
    1. Shakespeare, William, 1564-1616. Merchant of Venice.
I. Title. II. Series.
PR2825.S68 1988
822.3'3--dc19   88-12005
                                                         CIP

This is volume 3 in the continuing series
Studies in British Literature
Volume 3 ISBN 0-88946-930-X
SBL Series ISBN 0-88946-927-X

The Edwin Mellen Press

Box 450   Box 67
Lewiston, New York   Queenston, Ontario
USA 14092   L0S 1L0 CANADA
                       Mellen House
                Lampeter, Dyfed, Wales
           UNITED KINGDOM SA48 7DY

Printed in the United States of America

Table of Contents

Preface

This book attempts to describe the genesis (coming into being) of Shakespeare's <u>Merchant of Venice</u>. It is a biography of the play before it made its debut on the stage. As such it studies <u>The Merchant</u>'s ancestors-- the sources, including plots, ideas, attitudes, proper names, character types, etc.--with attention to what they apparently did and did not contribute and how they were modified and arranged to form the play's character. The intention is to provide insight into the craft and meaning of <u>The Merchant</u>.

Each generation since 1700 has seen the play's most interesting character Shylock in terms of its own attitudes, and the sum of their criticism has enriched the character well beyond even what the playwright created. A number of these interpretations from the mature life of the play are discussed in the final chapter, but a few that seem to inhibit understanding of its genesis receive attention earlier (e.g., the skeptical notion that Shakespeare had Portia deliberately hint to Bassanio which casket he should choose, and the sentimental suggestion that Shylock sincerely means to be friends with Antonio when he proposes the flesh bond). For the most part, however, the focus is on the elements that went into the play from the viewpoint of Shakespeare, an adapter of plots and creator of characters, as he prepared what may have been his fourteenth play for his company of actors to present to their London audience in the late 1590s.

My study of Shakespeare's <u>Merchant</u> and its sources, text, annotation, stage history, and criticism began in 1967-68 at the Folger Shakespeare Library and the British Museum Library. It was supported by the generosity of the Guggenheim Foundation in granting me a Fellowship and by a Research Leave from Illinois State University. More recently my research has been supported by the University of North Carolina at Greensboro, including a Research Assignment for 1985-86 to prepare the manuscript of this book. In addition to the Guggenheim Foundation and the two universities and two libraries referred to above, I am grateful to Dr. James Thompson and the Jackson Library at the University of North Carolina at Greensboro and also to the Libraries of Illinois State University and the University of Illinois. I wish to thank Professor G. Blakemore Evans and the late Dr. James G. McManaway for their early support of this research. Marie Soyars has word processed the manuscript. And first, last, and always my thanks are due to Dorothy.

March, 1988

THE GENESIS OF SHAKESPEARE'S
MERCHANT OF VENICE

Christopher Spencer

Chapter I
Introduction

The flesh-bond story, the earliest extant version
of which was written about four centuries before The
Merchant of Venice, seems to have had two main at-
tractions for Shakespeare. One was the opportunity to
develop a story of friendship and of love, with the two
relationships in potential conflict but brought to an
harmonious conclusion without the loss of either. The
second attraction was the invitation and challenge to
develop the character of the Jew to rival the exotic,
theatrical creation of Christopher Marlowe in Barabas,
the Jew of Malta, whom Edward Alleyn had been playing
successfully on the stage for the rival Lord Admiral's
Men.[1]   Implicitly, there was also the challenge of
doing both in the same play while at the same time
submitting both to the demands of the fantastic flesh-
bond story itself.

Friendship--often in conflict with heterosexual
love--was a favorite theme of the Renaissance, and it
was a theme which Shakespeare had used previously.
Around 1594, some three years before he wrote The
Merchant, he had composed a comedy of love and
friendship in The Two Gentlemen of Verona, calling

attention to the friendship in the title as he was to name The Merchant of Venice after one of the friends, Antonio. Furthermore, during the 1590s Shakespeare wrote The Sonnets, in which he explored at length and with great sensitivity the friendship between a mature, established, older man and a younger, noble, unsettled man, who is urged to marry, and who, though he is apparently responsive to the older man, does little but receive the latter's affection. In these broad ways earlier works provided suggestions for developing the friendship-love theme in the flesh-bond story.

Love and friendship are elegantly balanced in The Merchant. At the beginning of the play Antonio departs from his usual custom of not borrowing money and, in the name of friendship, borrows from a man he hates and despises to help his young friend Bassanio leave him for Belmont to win Portia. The bond is a pound of flesh. After the lady is won, she postpones the consummation of her marriage in order to send her husband to Venice to rescue Antonio from his enemy; she offers to pay whatever is necessary to save him, and she herself follows Bassanio, contributing her own time, effort, and ingenuity to the successful rescue. When, disguised as the victorious young lawyer, she asks her husband to grant her the ring she had given him as a symbol of their love, Bassanio declines because of his vow never to give it away; but when the friend Antonio urges him to do so, he sends it after the lawyer, thus placing the claims of friendship above those of love (though since he is unknowingly returning the ring to his wife, he does not in fact succeed in doing so).

Later, Portia torments Bassanio for surrendering the ring, but finally she symbolizes her forgiveness by passing it back to her husband through the hands of the friend. It is a bond among the three of them:

Ant. . . . I dare be bound again,
My soul upon the forfeit, that your lord
Will never more break faith advisedly.
Por. Then you shall be his surety. Give him this,
And bid him keep it better than the other.
Ant. Here, Lord Bassanio, swear to keep this ring.
(5.1.251-56).[2]

Thus, the friend has supported the claims of love self-sacrificingly for the first half of the play, and the lovers have saved the friend in the second half, Act 3, Scene 2 being both the high point of the love story and the point of reversal where the obligation passes from Antonio to Portia. Each friend has acknowledged the claims of love (Bassanio by seeking Portia, and Antonio by borrowing from an enemy to make the courtship possible), and each lover has acknowledged the claims of friendship (Bassanio by giving up the ring at his friend's request, and Portia by saving Antonio and forgiving Bassanio for putting his friend's wishes first). Portia gladly passes the ring to Antonio, who gladly passes it to Bassanio, who gladly wears it.

In molding the flesh-bond story into its shape as a finished play with a friendship-love theme, Shakespeare attempted to remove several flaws in the plot that had appeared in most or all of the earlier versions of the tale, such as the unworthiness of the suitor, the scandalous behavior of the lady, the reconciliation of borrower and lender, and the improbability of the flesh-bond itself. He was successful in some of these efforts, only partially so in others. He also created new problems for himself by

developing the friendship-love theme and by making the
Jew into a dynamic character, more substantial than the
others in the play. The sympathetic portrayal in depth
of <u>relationships</u> in opposition to the powerful and
understanding development of the <u>character</u> who is the
antagonist stretches the story in conflicting
directions.

Chapter II below analyzes the earlier versions of
the bond story. Since the direct source of the play
may not be extant, and since the story was widely
known, so that the playwright could have encountered
several versions orally, all earlier flesh-bond tales
seem relevant to a study of <u>The Merchant</u>. Moreover, if
the direct source has not survived, the writer of that
unknown source may have encountered several of the
surviving versions himself that would then have been
indirect sources of Shakespeare's play. Chapter III
considers other plot elements, such as the caskets
story and the stealing of the Jew's daughter, as well
as some influences of <u>The Two Gentlemen of Verona</u> and
<u>The Sonnets</u>. The thrust of the discussion in these two
chapters is to trace the genesis of the bond plot as it
grows in other hands, evolves from the earlier
versions, and is combined with other material to form
the full plot of Shakespeare's play.

Chapter IV takes the development of <u>The Merchant</u>
beyond the sources of the story as it considers the
characters Shakespeare added that are not essential to
the plot and some reasons for their presence. Then it
discusses the three main characters who play the
essential roles in the friendship-love theme, Antonio,
Bassanio, and Portia. The names of the characters,
none of which come from extant sources of the plot, are
often keys to their roles. Chapter V examines the

structure of <u>The Merchant</u> from the point of view of the dramatist's selection and arrangement of scenes and climaxes.

Chapters VI through VIII focus on Shylock. Chapter VI discusses the contemporary background material for Jews and usurers in Elizabethan England, which is the major "source" of the character and guide to the context in which the playwright assumed the character would be understood. It then analyzes the word <u>Jew</u> as it is used in the play, especially in the stage directions and speech ascriptions in the First Quarto (1600), and its significance for understanding Shakespeare's intentions. With a detailed discussion of the scene in which Shylock is introduced and the bond made (1.3) as well as the courtroom scene (4.1), Chapter VII argues that Shakespeare's presentation of Shylock is governed by the needs of the plot, especially the need to make the bond and Shylock's serious pursuit of it seem real, rather than by a desire to say anything about Jews or to create a conventional kind of character, such as a comic or a serious villain. Chapter VIII surveys criticism of Shylock in the light of Chapter VII's conclusions and attempts to answer two major questions: how should the role of Shylock be interpreted, and why is the portrayal of Shylock as vivid as it is?

Before we proceed something should be said about the probable date of <u>The Merchant</u> and about the early texts of the play. As John Russell Brown has shown, <u>The Merchant</u> was probably written between July of 1596, when the Spanish ship, the <u>St. Andrew</u>, was captured and run aground (an event alluded to in 1.1.27-29), and July of 1598, when <u>The Merchant</u> was entered in the <u>Stationers Register</u> by the printer James Roberts.[3]

Studies of the development of Shakespeare's style and versification generally confirm this conclusion.

The First Quarto (Q1) was published by Thomas Heyes in 1600 after he had reentered the play in the Stationers Register, recording Roberts' permission to publish it and also using Roberts as the printer.[4] Two compositors set the type, the same two who were responsible for the Second Quarto of Hamlet (1604) and whose habits are fairly well known.[5] There was a Second Quarto (1619, but falsely dated 1600 on the title page) and a Third in 1637. Both were printed from Q1. The text of The Merchant in the First Folio (1623) was also printed from Q1 with a few changes apparently from a Jacobean prompt book. The Second (1623), Third (1663-64), and Fourth (1685) Folios each repeated the text of its predecessor, making a few unauthoritative corrections and introducing new errors. The first edited text of The Merchant was published by Nicholas Rowe in 1709. The quartos do not provide either act or scene divisions for the play. Act divisions were first supplied in the First Folio and the conventional scene divisions by Rowe and later eighteenth-century editors.

Q1 is, then, the authoritative edition. It provides a good, relatively error-free text of the play. Its characteristics, including descriptive stage directions and inconsistent handling of proper names, have led scholars to think that it was printed from a "fair copy" of Shakespeare's manuscript, perhaps in his own hand.[6] Some of the points made below receive support if Q1 was printed from Shakespeare's manuscript; at the same time, some of them, especially the variation between Iew and Shy in Shylock's speech

prefixes, lend support to the view that the copy for Q1
was indeed a manuscript very close to Shakespeare's.

Chapter II
The Genesis of the Flesh-Bond Plot

The origins of the pound-of-flesh story have been traced to the Mahabharata (c. 300 BC) in the Far East, to the Talmud (also c. 300 BC) in the Middle East, and to the Twelve Tables of the Roman Law (codified, according to tradition, c. 451-52 BC) in Europe.[1] According to the indirect evidence that exists about the latter, Legis Actio per Manus Injectionem permitted the creditor to bring the debtor before a magistrate after thirty days' grace. If the debtor could not pay the obligation and nobody would pay for him, the creditor could put him in chains for sixty days, but must see that he was fed and must bring him before the praetor on three consecutive market days, when the amount of the debt was proclaimed. If the debt was still unpaid at the end of sixty days, the debtor could be sold to a foreigner across the Tiber or he could be killed or the creditors (if there were more than one) could divide his body among them.[2] Shakespeare does not allude to this law, and the earliest extant version of the bond story dates from c. 1200 AD. Nevertheless, late medieval and Renaissance examples may have been descended from the Roman law.

No doubt the story developed orally during the first twelve centuries of the Christian era. Living close to violence, cruelty, and physical mutilation--sometimes mutilation by legal process--people probably found the story less fantastic than we do. The defeat of the cruel usurer would have been satisfying, and in versions where the usurer was also a Jew, medieval Christian audiences must have had an even more enthusiastic response.

Our discussion of the bond plot will analyze the seven pre-Shakespearean versions that are extant and will include also brief comment on a few medieval plays and The Three Ladies of London, dramatic works that include trial scenes in which Jews attempt to collect debts from Christian merchants. The bond story was widely known. Written in several languages and countries, each of the seven represents a different genre: anecdote, story of the true cross, religious allegory, ballad, Italian novella, Euphuistic novel, and sample declamation. The medieval plays and The Three Ladies represent still another genre, the drama. The works are as follows:

Dolopathos by Johannes de Alta Silva (c. 1200), an anecdote in Latin prose.

Cursor Mundi (c. 1290), an English verse story of the true cross.

Medieval mystery, miracle, and morality plays that include trial scenes (1300-1600), French and English.

Gesta Romanorum (British Museum Harleian MS 7333, c. 1450), a religious allegory in English prose.

The Three Ladies of London by R[obert]
W[ilson] (performed by Leicester's Men c. 1581 and
printed 1584), an English play.

Gernutus (probably 1567-80, printed 1610), an
English ballad.

Il Pecorone, First Story, Fourth Day, by
Giovanni Fiorentino (1378, published in Italy,
1558), an Italian novella.

Zelauto or the Fountaine of Fame by Anthony
Munday (1580), an English Euphuistic novel.

The Orator, Discourse 95, by L[azarus] P[iot]
(1596), a pair of courtroom declamations.

Since the first three had apparently not been printed
by Shakespeare's time, it is unlikely that he read them
although, as noted above, he may have heard or heard of
them orally.

Doubtless there were other versions. It has been
suggested that Shakespeare had as his most immediate
source a play that has not survived. There are as many
as three specific candidates. First, in 1579 Stephen
Gosson referred to a play called "The Jew" performed at
the Bull and "representing the greedinesse of worldly
chusers, and bloody mindes of Usurers."[3] These phrases
may suggest the failure of Morocco and Arragon to
choose the right casket and the villainy of the money-
lender, or they may both refer to the greed and cruelty
of the usurer. Second, in 1653 a play called The Jew
of Venice by Thomas Dekker (c. 1572-1632) was entered
in the Stationers Register (but was apparently never
printed). And third, Philip Henslowe recorded twelve
performances of a "venesyon comodey" between August of
1594 and May of the following year. Although Dekker's
dates prevent identification of the first with the
second, the first or second references might be to the

play Henslowe mentions.[4]   Unfortunately, barring new evidence, we cannot know whether one or more of these works told the flesh-bond story, but the existence of these lost plays reminds us that other dramas on Jews and Venice did exist.

The earliest extant version of the flesh-bond story is in Johannes de Alta Silva's Dolopathos (c. 1200) in Latin prose and a French verse translation by Herbers, le Clerc (Li Romans di Dolopathos) a few years later.[5]   Dolopathos seems to be the "oldest western form" of the forty or so extant versions of the Seven Sages of Rome cycle of stories.[6]   The pound-of-flesh story is the fourth of eight tales told by seven wise men and Virgil on successive days to postpone King Dolopathos of Sicily's wrongful execution of his son. Its moral is that "life and death, freedom and condemnation [differ] by only a needle's point"; in Gilleland's translation it is about one thousand words in length.

A wise, young noblewoman, skilled in magic and determined to marry a man as wise and noble as she, allows suitors to try to sleep with her on payment of one hundred marks of silver. If she and the suitor please each other, they are to be married; but she always puts her would-be husbands to sleep with a magic owl's feather beneath the pillow. A certain noble but poor suitor who has previously failed borrows the sum for a year for a second attempt from a rich slave (not a Jew) whose foot he has cut off previously in a fit of anger. The bond is the weight of the silver in flesh and bones. Succeeding by accidentally displacing the feather, the suitor marries the lady and forgets the bond. When the creditor attempts to collect, the king is unable to persuade him to accept money in lieu of

the flesh; but the lover is saved by the lady, who
disguises herself as a lawyer and changes her voice by
magic. She limits the creditor to not "a needle's
point more or less than the just weight" and forbids
him to shed a drop of blood. The creditor not only
declines to take the flesh but also presents the lover
with another thousand marks for his friendship.

In an anecdote, character and probability are not
the point; it is success, the ingenious trick or device
that results in the total defeat of the villain, and
perhaps the rather strained moral that matter.
However, the flaws that mar the story in later hands
are glaringly apparent in Dolopathos. The lover's
borrowing from an enemy on dangerous terms is highly
improbable, and the vengeful creditor's gift at the end
(the reconciliation) is incredible. The lover's
behavior—not only borrowing the money from an enemy at
risk to his life, but also displacing the feather only
by accident, and forgetting the bond of his own flesh—
hardly demonstrates the wisdom the lady was seeking in
a husband. From a romantic viewpoint it is distressing
that the lady has been increasing her wealth for some
time by a dubious invitation and an unfair trick. The
last problem is solved brilliantly in The Merchant with
the casket story. Shakespeare works hard to make the
borrowing from an enemy believable, but his success (as
we shall see) comes at the price of new difficulties
with the "reconciliation" at the end of the courtroom
scene. Despite the opportunity Bassanio has to prove
himself with the caskets, many readers and critics have
complained that he is an undeserving romantic hero.

The next version to survive, the first in English,
is in Cursor Mundi, from around 1290, the year in which
Jews were banished from England for, as it turned out,

365 years.[7] The money-lender is a Jew, and the bond story may preserve the nation's memory of attitudes around the time of the expulsion. Although it had not been printed by Shakespeare's day, and there is no particular reason to suppose that Shakespeare had read it, the version in Cursor Mundi stands for similar tales that may have circulated orally. It is no longer than the version in Dolopathos, but there is no love story; the scene is at the court of Queen Eline, the mother of the Emperor Constantine, until it moves to Calvary.

Two messengers, who have come from Constantine to his mother in their search for the true cross, are assigned to decide the trial of a Christian goldsmith, who must make up the weight of gold he cannot repay to the Jew with his flesh. The Jew rejects ransom, has a sharp knife in his hand, and declares that he will take the goldsmith's eyes first, then his hand, his nose, and finally the rest to make up the amount. After he is defeated by being warned that he must shed no blood, the Jew is told he must forfeit his goods and lose his tongue. This punishment is not imposed when he reveals the burying place of the true cross, and its discovery and the miracles it performs lead to the baptism of many Jews. No motive is provided for the Jew's vicious cruelty; presumably it was enough for its time that he is a Jew. The conversion of the Jews anticipates the conversion forced on Shylock at the end of the courtroom scene in The Merchant.

Once the bond plot opposed Christian and Jew, especially in the context of a trial, a mass of dramatic literature from the Middle Ages became relevant, including miracle plays, mystery play cycles, and moralities. Davis and Richards discuss French miracle plays having trial scenes with reference to Shakespeare's play. In Le Miracle de un marchant et un juif (1377) the generous merchant Audry, who is a good servant to the Virgin Mary, exhausts his substance and borrows a thousand livres from the Jew Moussé, agreeing to become the latter's slave if he fails to repay the debt. After Audry becomes successful again, he forgets the debt until the last moment; then he puts the gold in a casket, places the casket in the sea, and trusts God to see that Moussé receives it in time. God obliges, but Moussé does not realize that the gold comes from Audry and later demands that Audry become his serf. God, accompanied by Gabriel, Michael, and the Virgin Mary, appears to testify for Audry, and Moussé, impressed, converts to Christianity. Davis and Richards refer to other similar dramas, pointing out that these plays "hint at a network of inter-relating stories, folk tales, and early drama from which Shakespeare may have drawn directly or indirectly" in The Merchant.[8] The love story is absent, and slavery replaces the pound of flesh; but here are the generous Christian merchant, the struggle of Christian against Jew with a miraculous rescue, and the reconciliation-conversion.

In the mystery play cycles there was often a play about conversion of the Jews dramatized from the popular medieval sermon, Contra Judaeos.[9] Moreover, common to both miracle and morality plays was a "trial" or debate in Heaven among the four daughters of God over the treatment to be accorded mankind: Justice and Truth in their harsher aspects represent the Old Testament view, demanding that man be damned, while Peace and Mercy, representing the New Law, plead for man's forgiveness.[10] The plea for mercy wins in the religious drama, as it does in <u>The Merchant</u>. Since mystery plays had continued to be performed into Shakespeare's lifetime,[11] and the influence of the moralities was strong in the Elizabethan theater, the playwright was working within traditions that may have been dying but were not yet dead.

The <u>Gesta Romanorum</u> was a widely known collection of stories (283 in all), with the contents varying in different manuscripts.[12] Among 166 manuscripts of the <u>Gesta</u>, Cardozo found the pound-of-flesh story in 24; 3 of the 24 were located in England, 2 in Latin and the other (Harleian MS 7333) in English. Of 28 editions <u>printed</u> on the Continent before 1558, only one (Augsburg, 1489) has the story, and no extant English edition from Shakespeare's time contains it.[13] Probably, then, Shakespeare did not read it; but the stories were widely known [14] and may well have reached him orally. The <u>Gesta</u> version is about twice as long as the <u>Dolopathos</u> story (two-and-one-half times including its allegorical application) and improves its predecessor with more detail. Most of the stories in the <u>Gesta</u> are followed by moral and allegorical applications, some of which, like this one, seem to modern readers to fit the stories very loosely indeed.

The fair daughter of the Roman Emperor Selestinus rejects a knight who loves her, saying she will not lie by him all night unless he gives her a hundred marks.[15] After twice having paid and fallen asleep instantly, the knight goes to a far city where he signs a charter with his own blood to borrow the money from an unknown merchant. His flesh is the bond. Then he visits Virgil the philosopher, who advises him to remove a magic letter from between the sheet and the coverlet when he next goes to bed with the lady. After

returning to the Emperor's daughter and following
Virgil's advice, feigning sleep until she comes to bed,
he makes love to her despite her protestations that she
is a virgin. He continues to sleep with the lady and
forgets the bond until it is fourteen days overdue.
When he remembers, the lady encourages him to seek out
the merchant and offer him double what is owed. The
merchant rejects the offer of money and has the debtor
arrested. Dressing as a knight, the lady follows her
lover, appears before the judge, and delivers the
debtor by forbidding the merchant to shed blood. When
the lover returns home, the lady taunts him for not
bringing the wise knight to dinner and then dons her
disguise to prove what had happened. The lover weeps;
they are married and "livid and deyde in the service of
god; and yelde to god goode sowlis."

The "Moralitee" that follows resembles most others
in the Gesta. The reader is told that the Emperor is
Jesus Christ; his daughter is the soul; the lover is
"every worldly man," who is night and day trying to
dirty his soul; the letter is the virtues that come
from baptism and prevent him for a time from success in
his foul intentions; the merchant is the Devil, who
delights in deadly sin and persuades the lover to sign
a charter with his blood. Virgil, who advised the
lover how to succeed in dirtying his soul, is pride of
life. The lady (the soul) casts off her old clothes
and puts on new to ride her palfrey (Reason) to the
courtroom (the church). She shows that we must over-
come flesh so that no blood falls, thereby defeating
the Devil and allowing flesh and spirit to be married
"to live in blisse."

This allegorical explanation makes irrelevant some
of the problems and improbabilities in more secular

versions of the story. The lover is undeserving and foolish in figuring out nothing for himself, in borrowing the money from a stranger at such risk, and in forgetting the bond, because the moral of the story demands that he be the conventional fleshly, foolish everyman, quick to forget his sins. The merchant's motives need not be explained because the Devil's motives are obvious, and no reconciliation with the Devil is expected or possible at the end of the story. The lady is above reproach, for she is the soul striving to remain pure at the expense of everyman, though she cannot escape from him; she is wise and knows the answer to the Devil when nobody else does because she is the daughter of Jesus Christ.

Shakespeare tells a much more realistic story with human beings, not symbolic figures. Yet, assuming some general familiarity with the _Gesta_ story in him and his audience, we might suppose that for them Shylock's being called a "devil" on several occasions was not an idle allusion, that Portia's delivering her mercy speech to a Jew before she supplies a solution that (improbably) has not occurred to anyone else is appropriate for someone whose literary ancestor was the daughter of Jesus Christ, and that Bassanio's choice among the caskets (based on another highly moral story from the _Gesta_) is indeed supposed to reveal as worthy a rather ordinary, everyday man. The _Gesta_ lady's behavior after the knight is freed--taunting him and proving that she had saved him--looks toward the more imaginative addition of the ring story in _Il Pecorone_ and _The Merchant of Venice_.

From Shakespeare's lifetime (c. 1581) the trial scene between Christian and Jew appears in an allegorical setting in _The Three Ladies of London_, by

R[obert] W[ilson].[16] The three ladies are Lucre, Love, and Conscience; with the aid of a number of symbolic persons (Dissimulation, Simony, Usury, etc.), Lady Lucre is dominating London and making life miserable for Lady Love and Lady Conscience. Mercatore, an Italian merchant, is anxious to serve Lady Lucre and is ordered by her to cheat a Jew named Gerontus, from whom he has borrowed a total of three thousand ducats (the exact amount that Antonio borrows from Shylock). Three scenes between Gerontus and Mercatore are set in Turkey, where the latter is brought to trial and where the law provides that anyone who converts to Moslem is forgiven his debts. The merchant offers to become a Mohammedan, and the Jew, horrified that one would forsake his faith merely for money, cancels the interest, then half the principal, and finally the whole debt--whereupon Mercatore decides to remain a Christian. The Judge concludes, "Jews seek to excel in Christianity and Christians in Jewishness,"[17] reminding one of Antonio's pun on gentle and gentile:

> Hie thee, gentle Jew.
> The Hebrew will turn Christian, he grows kind.
> (1.3.177-78).

It is noteworthy that the play is about money and that the Jew is presented as a man who respects principle, whereas the merchant spectacularly does not. (However, the Jew is merely a means of satirizing the unscrupulous Christian; there is no attempt to make him a sympathetic or attractive figure.) Even if The Three Ladies was no longer being played in London after Shakespeare's arrival there between 1588 and 1592, the play was in print (1584), and there is no difficulty in supposing that Shakespeare read it or heard about it. Bullough prints selections as an "analogue."[18]

In the first stanza of the ballad Gernutus it is said that "Italian writers" have told the story, but the title (which is the name of the Jew) sounds sufficiently like "Gerontus" that a connection between it and The Three Ladies has been suggested.[19] If Hyder Rollins is correct in thinking that the extant text of Gernutus, which was published around 1610, is a reprint of an older ballad of 1567-80, the ballad probably preceded the play.[20] Gernutus is in 41 four-line stanzas (or 82 fourteeners) and is set in Venice. As "a merry ieast" (compare Shylock's "merry sport," 1.3.145), the Jewish usurer Gernutus lends a merchant ("being distressed in his need") one hundred crowns for a year.[21] The bond is a pound of flesh. After the merchant's ships are lost, Gernutus pretends to be generous until the bond is past due. When he brings the merchant to trial, the Jew is defeated by the Judge, who threatens him with hanging if he sheds blood or takes more or less than a pound of flesh. No motive is given for the Jew's cruelty, and there is no reconciliation.

The ballad concludes with the warning

> That many a wretch as ill as he
>   doth live now at this day,
>
> That seeketh nothing but the spoyle
>   of many a wealthie man,
> And for to trap the innocent,
>   deviseth what they can.

Evidently, Gernutus is to be taken as a warning against usurers more than against Jews. Bullough thinks that Shakespeare may have known the ballad, though he does

not include it in his selection.[22]   Again, Shakespeare
may have heard or heard of this story and its moral
rather than read it.

About two hundred years before Gernutus, Giovanni
Fiorentino wrote Il Pecorone (1378); it was published
in Milan in 1558, six years before Shakespeare was
born.   If the First Story of the Fourth Day was not
known to Shakespeare, its parent, sibling, or
descendant must have been, and Il Pecorone must serve
as proxy for Shakespeare's most important source of the
bond plot, if it was not the real thing.   Giovanni's
story is set in Belmonte and Venice, as is
Shakespeare's, and it includes the story of the ring
returned by the lover to the lady in disguise, her
taunting him about it, and her returning it to prove
that she was the clever lawyer.   No other extant
version of the story uses the name "Belmont" or
includes the ring story.   The Italian novella also has
an elderly debtor (the lover's godfather and guardian),
and the Lady of Belmonte has a maid who, like Nerissa,
is married at the end.   Bernard Grebanier lists thirty-
three "echoes" of Il Pecorone in The Merchant, which,
he thinks, "indicate the great probability that
Shakespeare read his Fiorentino in Italian."[23]
Collectively, the verbal parallels are certainly
suggestive, though they could have developed
independently or have reached the dramatist through an
intermediary.   We do not know whether Shakespeare read
Italian, but the language in the Italian story is so
simple that a person who knows Latin and French can
grasp the plot readily by skimming.[24]   There may have
been a translation that has not survived, or a person
who had read the story may have told the playwright
about it.

The Italian _novella_ is about 7500 words in length, more than seven times the length of the story in _Dolopathos_; it is roughly one-third as long as _The Merchant_. Giovanni's purpose is entirely to entertain, and he succeeds. His focus is on the young lover Giannetto; the only other named characters are his father Bindo (who dies in the first paragraph) and his godfather Ansaldo, who borrows the money. The Lady of Belmont, her servant, and the Jew are unnamed and not much developed as characters.

After his father's death in Florence, Giannetto goes to his godfather Ansaldo in Venice, who gives him money generously and encourages him to spend lavishly so that he will become popular. Giannetto succeeds: "he behaved so wisely, that almost all Venice thought well of him, seeing him to be so wise, with such charm and courtesy beyond measure; indeed the ladies and gentlemen seemed in love with him, and Ansaldo had eyes for none but him, so pleased was he with his style and manner. There was scarcely a party in Venice to which Giannetto was not invited, so much was everyone fond of him."[25] Two of this popular young man's friends make an annual voyage to Alexandria to sell their goods, and Ansaldo equips a fine ship for Giannetto to join them.

After several days' sailing, they pass a bay with a fine port. The ship's captain explains that the ruler of the port is a widow, "'a beautiful and charming lady, and she makes this law--that anyone who arrives there must agree to sleep with her, and if he can enjoy her, to take her as his wife and be lord of the port and of all the country. But if he cannot enjoy her, he loses all he has.'" Giannetto slips away from his friends and enters the harbor. He is welcomed and pleases everyone with his "good manners, pleasant personality, and conversation"; they party all day, "and everyone would have been pleased to have him as their lord." When the lady takes him to her chamber, she gives him sweetmeats and wine that is drugged so that he falls asleep. The following morning she confiscates his richly laden ship but lets him have a horse and expense money to return to Venice, where he claims that he lost his ship when it struck a rock. Thinking continually of the Lady of Belmont, Giannetto becomes melancholy, and the following year Ansaldo equips another ship so that the young man can again accompany his friends to Alexandria. Again he steals away to Belmont, where he is welcomed, is drugged in the same manner as before, loses his ship, returns to Venice, lies about his loss, cannot put the lady out of his mind, and becomes melancholy.

The third time Ansaldo lacks sufficient capital to equip the ship in proper style, and since he needs ten thousand ducats, he goes to a "Jew at Mestri" and borrows them on condition that if he does not repay them by St. John's Day in the following June, the Jew can "take from him a pound of flesh from whatever part of his body he pleased." Ansaldo signs the agreement, which is properly witnessed. Before Giannetto leaves, Ansaldo asks "'one favor--that if misfortune befalls you, you please come to visit me, so that I may see you before I die, and I will be content.'" (This reminds one of Antonio's request, "all debts are clear'd between you and I, if I might but see you at my death," 3.2.318-20.) Giannetto is welcome again at Belmont, and a tournament is held in his honor, at which he excels. When he goes to the Lady's bedroom, the maid whispers, "'Pretend to drink, but do not drink this evening.'" So warned, Giannetto "pour[s the drink]

into his bosom," goes to bed and snores. When the Lady
joins him, he gives her "the peace of holy matrimony."
The Lady is "more than content," and there are great
festivities at the marriage. Giannetto rules well but
forgets Ansaldo until he is reminded by the festivities
of St. John's Day. When he tells the Lady what has
happened, she urges him to return to Venice
immediately, and he does so, "taking twenty followers
and a large amount of money." The Jew has had Ansaldo
arrested, but gives him a few days' grace to wait for
Giannetto, though he says he will take the flesh anyway
"to be able to say that he had put to death the
greatest merchant among the Christians."

The Lady follows her husband, "dressed as a judge,
with two attendants." Since Venice is "a city of law,"
Giannetto and the merchants can only plead with the
Jew, who rejects offers of twenty, thirty, forty,
fifty, and finally one hundred thousand ducats. He
says he would not accept "'more ducats than this city
is worth . . . ; I wish to do what my bond says.'" At
this point the Lady arrives at an inn in Venice and is
introduced by her servant as "a gentleman-judge" from
Bologna. She is told about Giannetto and Ansaldo and
promises an easy solution. When the case is taken to
her, she warns the Jew to take the money he has been
offered, but he refuses. Ansaldo is stripped, and the
Jew prepares his razor. At the last moment, the Lady
says, "'Be careful what you do, for if you take more or
less than a pound, I will have your head cut off. And
I tell you further, that if you spill a little drop of
blood, I shall have you put to death; for your bond
does not make mention of the shedding of blood, but
instead says that you may take a pound of flesh from
him, and it does not say more or less.'" The Jew is

then willing to accept first one hundred thousand ducats, then ninety thousand, and so on to ten thousand. When he is told he can have only the pound of flesh, he tears the bond angrily and departs. There is no conversion or reconciliation.

The Lady rejects the money she is offered by Giannetto and asks instead for his ring, which he reluctantly but on his own initiative gives up. After celebrations in Venice Giannetto takes Ansaldo to Belmont, where the Lady, "pretending that she had been to the baths," has preceded him. She welcomes the godfather but pretends to be angry with her husband, whom she accuses of giving the ring to his mistresses. When Giannetto says he gave it to the Judge, she asserts that a woman received it. But when he weeps she repents and shows him the ring. Rejoicing, Giannetto gives the Lady's maid, who had warned him about the drink, to Ansaldo as wife, and Giannetto and the Lady live "for a long time in happiness and joy, while their lives lasted."

Il Pecorone and The Merchant are alike in combining an affectionate relationship between an older and a younger man, a courtship story involving a challenge, and the ring story with the flesh-bond plot. In his love for Bassanio even to the point of sacrificing his life and in his willingness to help the young man again and again, the rich Venetian merchant Ansaldo is like Antonio. And Giannetto's popularity, his having spent freely in the past, and his desire to visit the Lady again suggest Bassanio. However, unlike Shakespeare's lover, Giannetto is flawed in that he lies to his benefactor about how he lost his ships and forgets the elderly debtor for some time after winning the Lady. There is much less of Il Pecorone in Portia and

Shylock. Like the Lady of Belmont, Portia is rich, beautiful, clever, and has a marriageable maid-servant, but she is a maiden in love rather than a widow and does not have the nasty way of adding to her fortune that the Lady employs. There is hardly anything of Shylock in Giovanni's shadowy Jew.

Zelauto the Fountaine of Fame (1580) by Anthony Munday is an English novel in the style made popular by John Lyly's Euphues two years earlier and mimicked by Shakespeare in the second scene of The Merchant. In Chapters V through VII of the Third Part Astraepho narrates a version of the bond story to Zelauto, the son of the Duke of Venice. The setting is Verona. Two young men, Strabino and Rodolfo, are in love, Strabino with Rodolfo's sister Cornelia, and Rodolfo with Brisana, who is the daughter of a Christian usurer Truculento; this usurer himself wants to marry Cornelia. Both fathers of the ladies withhold permission to marry, and the young men borrow 4000 ducats for one month from the usurer-father in order to buy a jewel that Cornelia's father covets so that he will change his mind. Although Rodolfo offers the "best lym of [his] body,"[26] Truculento successfully demands all their lands and their right eyes as the bond. Through ingenious trickery the marriages take place. When the young men are unable to repay the ducats on time, the usurer forgives them their estates but demands their right eyes; he rejects a late payment of any amount. After a series of long speeches at the trial (in which the two women appear disguised as lawyers), Cornelia defeats the usurer by threatening him with the loss of both his own eyes if he sheds a drop of blood. The usurer makes his new son-in-law his heir.

Scholars have emphasized the vigorous dialogue of the story and have suggested that it was based on a play.[27]   They have also noticed parallels with The Merchant of Venice: this is the only pre-Shakespearean version of the bond story in which the usurer has a daughter; the trial scene is fully developed (it is almost as long as Shakespeare's); the two women are disguised as lawyers; and the concluding emphasis is on inheritance by the usurer's son-in-law. Brown and Muir note that earlier in Munday's book the phrases "fare well frost" and "a cold sute" appear five sentences apart, and then, some pages later "a colde sute" appears in the same sentence as "loose no more labour."[28] These phrases occur in the last line of the scroll Morocco finds in the gold casket and his response to it:

> Fare you well, your suit is cold.
> Cold indeed, and labor lost:
> Then farewell heat, and welcome frost!
>   (2.7.73-75).

On the other hand, since the usurer is not a Jew, there is no conflict between Christian and Jew; the friendship is between two young men; the lovers themselves are the debtors; there is no Belmont contrasted with Venice; and technically there is no pound of flesh. Bullough lists Zelauto as a "possible source" for The Merchant.   Grebanier suggests reasonably that Shakespeare "read Munday's tale years earlier, and may have unconsciously remembered a detail or two."[29] Perhaps the remembering was not entirely unconscious.

The bond story appears in debate form in Declamation 95 of The Orator: Handling a hundred severall Discourses, in forme of Declamations: . . .

Written in French by Alexandre Silvayn, and Englished
by L. P. (London, 1596). Alexandre Silvayn is
Alexandre van den Busche (c. 1535-c. 1585), and L. P.
is "Lazarus Piot," whom Douce identified as Anthony
Munday, though the attribution is rejected by Munday's
biographer, Celeste Turner.[30] Declamation 95 is set in
Turkey and consists of two speeches, one by a Jew who
has been threatened with death if he collects either
more or less than his pound of flesh from a Christian
merchant (who owes him 900 crowns), and the second by
the Christian merchant in rebuttal. Some of the Jew's
arguments suggest Shylock's: his assertion that one
must not "breake the credite of trafficke amongst men
without great detriment unto the Commonwealth" is a
point made by both Antonio (3.3.26-31) and Shylock
(4.1.38-9), and his insistence that no further reason
for demanding the pound of flesh is needed beyond the
obligation itself is also a point made by Shylock.
L. P.'s Jew also argues that taking a pound of flesh is
a lesser thing than such common punishments as
imprisonment or slavery; Shylock does not offer this
argument, but he employs the example of "many a
purchas'd slave" that the Venetians own and use as they
please because they "bought them" to maintain his right
to the flesh he has purchased. The other arguments
from the Jew's speech would only have embarrassed
Shakespeare: that the Christian should cut and deliver
the pound of flesh himself as the debtor customarily
delivers his obligation (thereby Shylock would not be
guilty of shedding blood), and that the law should not
prevent the Jew from taking less than a pound.

The Christian's reply is less relevant to
Shakespeare's play. He argues that he was merely late
in delivering the money, that he suspects the Jew of

hindering him, that the Jew's insistence on flesh over money shows that his motive is merely hatred of Christians, and that the abominations, adulteries, and murders of the Old Testament are evidence that the Jews are an unworthy race. The attitude implied by the last point suggests the Antonio of 1.3, who hates Jews according to Shylock (1.3.48) and who calls him "dog" and spits on him (1.3.111-12). Muir thinks The Orator was a source for The Merchant; Bullough acknowledges that Shakespeare may have seen it but describes it as an "analogue."[31] One or both of these last two works-- Zelauto or The Orator--may have suggested to Shakespeare the possibilities of the courtroom scene.

To recapitulate: the elements of the flesh-bond plot, the relationships among the characters, and some details are likely to have reached Shakespeare-- directly or indirectly, in oral or in written form-- from the versions discussed above. From Dolopathos originally came the noblewoman, won through a test by the lover who puts up his flesh as surety to borrow the money to win her and who is then rescued by the disguised noblewoman, who insists on the exact weight and forbids the shedding of blood; the lender is then reconciled with the borrower. Cursor Mundi makes the lender a Jew, with the religious conflict that such a change entails (including conversion at the end). Medieval drama provides more examples of the religious conflict in a trial scene, though without using the flesh-bond story.

The Gesta version omits the Jew but develops symbolic religious implications of the love story and adds the realistic detail (potentially good theater) of the Lady's treatment of her husband after the trial. The Three Ladies presents a Jew without prejudice in a

trial contest against a Christian, with criticism of
the latter. With an economic emphasis, _Gernutus_ warns
against _usurers_ who falsely treat bonds as "merry
ieasts." _Il Pecorone_ develops a strong friendship
between an older man and a young lover, with the self-
sacrificing, older man making the bond; it has style,
develops the friends' characters, supplies the name
Belmont, and provides the story of the rings. _Zelauto_
gives the story an Euphuistic style, _two_ women
disguised as lawyers, and a lengthy and dramatic
courtroom scene. _The Orator_ offers further inspiration
for the courtroom scene, as well as two arguments that
Shakespeare emphasizes.

Chapter III
Other Sources and Influences

The practicalities of the Elizabethan stage and the conventions of romantic comedy required that Shakespeare (or a predecessor)[1] find a new way for the lady to be won. The previous versions of the story (except _Zelauto_) associate the lady with immorality and trickery, while the man succeeds eventually through luck or good advice but no virtue of his own. The lovers are actuated by sex and greed, not by romantic love. Moreover, to be effective in the theater the scenes of the lovers' failure and success in bed would have to take place on or just off stage, and such scenes are not common in Elizabethan drama--to say nothing of Shakespeare's romantic comedy. The caskets story is a brilliant solution to the problem: it is moral (even emphatically so) and straightforward (except to those critics who think Portia cheats); it enables the lover to make a wise choice (except to the aforementioned critics); and it is eminently stage-worthy.

It is generally agreed that the casket story came from the English translation of the _Gesta Romanorum_ originally published by Wynkyn de Worde (c. 1510) and revised and published by Richard Robinson in at least six editions (1577-1601); in the 1595 edition it is History 32.[2] Thus, it would have been readily available to Shakespeare, his predecessors, and his audience (unfortunately, Robinson did not include the bond story in his selection).

There were also many other versions of the casket plot available, though none so close to The Merchant. In Barlaam and Josephat (9th century), a king invites his nobles to choose among four chests, two covered with gold but filled with human bones and two covered with pitch but filled with precious stones, the moral being that one must not judge by appearances.[3] In Day 10, Story 1 of Boccaccio's Decameron (1353, published 1471), Ruggieri must choose between two identical coffers, one filled with riches and the other with earth, the moral emphasizing the gifts of Fortune. In Book V of his Confessio Amantis John Gower tells the story twice, first with two identical coffers to illustrate the evil of greed and the importance of Fortune and then with two identical pasties to show that serving God is superior to serving the king.[4] Shakespeare was to use Book VIII of the Confessio Amantis in Pericles and perhaps had already done so for The Comedy of Errors.[5] However, in none of the versions except History 32 in the Gesta are there inscriptions on the caskets.

In Robinson's translation of History 32 the King of Ampluy's daughter is tested to see whether she is worthy of marrying the Emperor of Rome's son. She must choose among three vessels: one gold engraved with the "posey" "Who so chooseth mee shall finde that he deserveth" but "full of dead mens bones"; one silver with the "superscription" "Who so chooseth me shall finde that his nature desireth" but "fylled with earthe and wormes"; and one lead whereon "was <u>insculpt</u> [emphasis added] this posey. Who so chooseth mee, shall finde that God hath disposed for him" but "full within of precious stones." The maiden rejects the gold because she is ignorant of the contents and the silver because she knows her "nature desireth the lust of the flesh." She chooses the lead because "God never disposed any harme," and she marries the Emperor's son. There follows the usual "Morall," that the Emperor's son is God's Son and the maiden is the soul. The gold vessel is worldly men and the dead men's bones the works that such men have wrought in this world, which are "dead in the sight of god"; in the silver vessel worms and earth represent the "faire speach" of "some Justices & wise men of this world," which shines but will not help them at the Day of Judgment; and the lead and precious stones stand for "a simple life and a poore, which the chosen men choose."

The choice in both History 32 and <u>The Merchant</u> is made to demonstrate worthiness for a noble marriage. The inscriptions on the vessels resemble those on Shakespeare's caskets, and Morocco uses the word "insculp'd" (2.7.57), apparently from Robinson's translation—the only appearance of the word in Shakespeare's works. The inscription on the <u>Gesta's</u> gold casket appears on Shakespeare's silver casket with little more alteration than the meter demands: "Who so chooseth mee shall finde that he deserveth" and "Who chooses me shall get as much as he deserves." The inscription on the <u>Gesta's</u> silver casket (concluding "that his nature desireth," i.e., the flesh), which is suitable in a medieval religious story that rejects the flesh, is altered on Shakespeare's gold casket to the

bland "what many men desire," more appropriate in a
Renaissance romantic comedy that does not wish to deny
the flesh. Since gold is more "desirable" than silver,
the inscriptions are exchanged, the other, emphasizing
"desert," being left for silver. As it happens,
Morocco receives both the skull ("dead mens bones") of
the Gesta's gold vessel and the reference to worms
("Gilded [tombs] do worms infold," 2.7.69) of the
silver vessel. The severity with which Morocco and
Arragon are dismissed may derive in part from the
absolute morality of the medieval source.

The inscription on the lead casket ceases to be
clearly religious: "that God hath disposed for him"
becomes "give and hazard all he hath," where Fortune
may preside (as in Boccaccio and Gower's first version)
or God may rule (as in the Gesta and Gower's second
version) or such specific questions need not arise. It
fits Bassanio in that he has risked all that he has
borrowed from Antonio, all that Antonio has borrowed
from Shylock, the life of his friend, his own
happiness, and the happiness of the woman he loves. In
the miraculous world of romantic comedy the inscription
on the lead casket seems written for Bassanio.

From the point of view of Portia's father, the
gold and silver caskets are supposed to eliminate
fortune-seekers and self-centered, proud suitors, as
well as those who do not care enough to risk choosing,
like the departing suitors described in 1.2. The lead
casket rewards the one who does not seek Portia's
wealth for itself and is sufficiently humble and right-
thinking (and perhaps shrewd) to receive the reward.
Knowing he does not "deserve" and that desiring is not
enough, Bassanio is willing to "hazard." The word
hazard is used eleven times in The Merchant, first by

Bassanio to Antonio (1.1.151), three times by Portia (2.1.45 to Morocco, 2.9.18 to Arragon, and 3.2.2 to Bassanio), three times as the inscription is read by the first two suitors, three times in six lines by Morocco (2.7.16-21), and once by Arragon as he rejects lead (2.9.22). The caskets support several morals—not judging by appearances, not being greedy, not being proud, and having the courage to "hazard"—to risk everything in order to win the lady.

Shakespeare builds up interest in the caskets ingeniously. They are mentioned briefly by Nerissa in the second scene of the play; they are discussed and the terms are made clearer by Morocco and Portia in 2.1, as Morocco complains about submitting to fortune— but still they are not shown. Six scenes later the curtains are drawn, revealing the caskets; the inscriptions are read twice to the audience; and the love of Bassanio and Portia is at risk as Morocco chooses—and chooses wrong, letting the audience know that gold is not the right choice. Two scenes later the curtain is drawn again; Arragon reads the inscriptions to the audience again; and the lovers are at risk again as Arragon chooses—and chooses wrong, letting the audience know that silver is also a wrong selection. In 3.2, having seen the caskets twice, knowing the inscriptions (which Bassanio does not repeat), and knowing that lead must be the right choice, the audience can largely ignore the caskets to focus on the agony and delight of the lovers, as Shakespeare postpones the climax by love poetry, song, and Bassanio's long speech as he chooses. Beyond its own fairy-tale drama, the sequence of scenes shows us Portia presiding with poise, courtesy, and wit; impresses us with her desirability; reveals to us

Bassanio triumphing over the mighty and the arrogant; stresses the moral or meaning of the choice in the three long speeches by the three suitors; and makes us, with Bassanio, almost forget Antonio back in Venice. It does make us forget the manner in which Giannetto and his predecessors won their women.

To the bond and casket plots Shakespeare (or, possibly, a predecessor) added the story of the Jewess who escapes from her father into marriage with a Christian. The idea may have come from Marlowe's Jew of Malta, where Abigail has a Christian lover and betrays her father, or from Munday's Zelauto, where the Christian usurer Truculento has his daughter stolen away from him. There are also other possibilities. Bullough prints a translation of the fourteenth tale in Masuccio di Salerno's Il Novellino (Naples, 1476) as a "probable source" and says of it,

> the elopement of Jessica came directly or
> indirectly from . . . Masuccio, which so far
> as we know, had not been translated into
> English. . . . Whether Shakespeare found it
> in a source-play or himself interwove it with
> the rest we cannot be sure; but he certainly
> gave it his own romantic tone.[6]

In Masuccio's tale, which is set in Naples, the cavalier of Messina, Giufreddi Saccano, sees and falls in love with a beautiful young lady who is shut up in her house by her avaricious (Christian) father. He becomes a friend of the father and introduces a female slave into the house who arranges the flight of the daughter with jewels and ducats. The lovers flee by boat and are married, while the avaricious father regrets the loss of jewels and ducats as much as the

loss of his daughter. The story provides the
avaricious father, the sequestered daughter, the
elopement with jewels, the helpful servant, and the
father's divided grief.

Masuccio's Story 14 lacks the important ingredient
that the father and daughter are not Jews. Beatrice D.
Brown provides a number of examples from the thirteenth
to the fifteenth century of "stories whose interest
centers in the love of a Christian youth for a Jewish
damsel." The closest to Shakespeare is in a
thirteenth-century collection of theological pieces: it
includes the "spendthrift" Christian lover, the fair
Jewess, the miserly old Jewish father, seduction and
robbery, conversion, and "the distribution of the
father's concern over both his grievances."[7] Like the
bond and casket plots, the story seems to have been
common knowledge.

In Marlowe's _Jew of Malta_ Barabas' daughter
Abigail appears in five scenes. In 1.2 she sympathizes
with her father's loss of his treasure, which is in the
house that the Christians have taken and turned into a
nunnery; she pretends to become a nun in order to gain
admittance. In 2.1 she appears "above" and throws the
gold and jewels down to Barabas. Abigail and the young
Christian Mathias are in love, and Mathias' friend, the
Governor's son Lodowick, upon seeing Abigail, falls in
love with her too. In 2.3 Barabas orders Abigail to
respond to Lodowick, whereupon Barabas so encourages
both young men that they fight and kill each other
(3.2). When Abigail despairingly decides to become a
nun (3.3), Barabas poisons her along with the entire
nunnery; but before she dies Abigail reveals to the
Christians that her father brought about the deaths of
Mathias and Lodowick (3.6).

Like Jessica, Abigail throws jewels from a balcony (but to, not from a Jew), loves a Christian, and turns against her father; but otherwise their stories have little in common. Barabas uses his daughter as an instrument first to save his treasure and then to destroy the Christian youths. Abigail provides a touch of sympathy for Barabas when he is trying to recover his treasure from the hypocritical Christians, but then she becomes the playwright's instrument for showing the cruelty and destructiveness of the Jew. Shakespeare has Jessica humanize Shylock by representing his home life, but she is opposed to him from the beginning and casts him in the heavy father role when she elopes with the jewels to irresponsible frivolities in Genoa (as Tubal tells us) and then to the Christian, responsible, ordered, beneficent society of Portia's Belmont. There she and her husband have the good fortune to become her father's heirs. Although the idea may have come from Marlowe, the development fits <u>The Merchant of Venice</u>.

Like Jessica, Launcelot, the Jew's servant, adds to the sense we have of Shylock's domestic establishment, is "saved" from the Jew, and is brought to Belmont. In Elizabethan literature usurers are often represented as being hard on their servants:[8] Launcelot asserts that he is "famish'd" in Shylock's house (2.2.106), and Shylock claims that he is "a huge feeder" (2.5.46). (Probably we are to understand that both are right.) The stage directions and speech prefixes in Q1 often call him "Clown," and it is generally assumed that Will Kempe, the actor of clown roles for the Lord Chamberlain's Men, originated the part.

Shakespeare borrowed Launcelot from his own earlier creation, Launce, the clown in <u>The Two</u>

Gentlemen of Verona. As Thomas B. Stroup points out, the name is a diminutive (perhaps double diminutive, Launce-l-et); he is "little Launce." Launcelet is often abbreviated to Launce in the speech prefixes of Q1 of The Merchant. Both characters entertain with clownish soliloquies as they act out the two sides of a dialogue; both roles offer opportunities for extempore acting; both characters are servants who leave home; and both ask blessings of their fathers. As Stroup suggests, the playwright seems to invite his audience to see Launcelot as a continuation of the earlier character.[9] Played by the same actor, possibly in a similar costume, the continuation would have been comically obvious on the stage.

Another borrowing from The Two Gentlemen is the arrangement of scenes in content and function in Acts I and II. Each play has three scenes in the first act. In the first scene the friends are introduced with emphasis on their separation: Valentine parts with Proteus as he leaves Verona for Milan, and Bassanio makes plans to leave Antonio and Venice for Belmont. In the second scene ladies are introduced: Julia's maid Lucetta describes her mistress's suitors, and Portia's maid Nerissa lists her mistress's suitors. In the third scene Proteus's father Antonio sends his son to visit Valentine (thereby moving the love scenes to Milan), while in The Merchant Antonio obtains from Shylock the means for Bassanio to go to Belmont, where the love scene will occur. Act II in The Two Gentlemen has seven scenes and The Merchant as traditionally divided has nine, though scenes three (or two) through six are often played as one. In both plays love scenes and would-be lovers alternate with clowns. True lovers in scenes one (Valentine/Silvia) and two (Proteus/

Julia) are followed by Launce in monologue and dialogue in three, a false lover (Thurio) in four, another clown scene in five, another false lover (Proteus for Silvia) in six, and finally in seven by Julia deciding in conversation with her maid to pursue Proteus disguised as a page. In The Merchant "false" lovers (Morocco and Arragon) appear in scenes one, seven, and nine; the clown is introduced by monologue and dialogue in two and continues in three through five; other lovers (Jessica and Lorenzo) dominate three through six; and Salerio and Solanio describe Bassanio's departure and Shylock's rage in eight.

Since the plots in the two plays are quite different, the parallels diminish as the plays advance. But there are still resemblances. As a rule there is a long, climactic scene in the third act of a Shakespeare play in which the characters' relationships and the direction of the action are significantly changed or even reversed. In The Two Gentlemen Proteus betrays Valentine to the Duke, and Valentine is separated from Silvia and banished to the forest (3.1), while in The Merchant Bassanio wins Portia but must immediately leave her for Venice to save his friend (3.2). In the earlier play Launce and Speed joke about Launcelot's woman (3.1), whereas in The Merchant Launcelot's joking with Lorenzo and Jessica includes the discovery that Launcelot's woman, the Moor, is pregnant (3.5). In 3.4 Portia parts with Lorenzo and jokes with Nerissa about adopting male disguise, as Julia had joked with Lucetta on the same subject in 2.7 of The Two Gentlemen.

There is little resemblance in Act 4: The Merchant reaches its major climax in the courtroom scene (4.1), while the four scenes in The Two Gentlemen prepare for the play's major climax in Act 5. Both dramas hurry to their conclusions: in four scenes and 256 lines the last act of <u>The Two Gentlemen</u> is the shortest final act in Shakespeare's plays, and in one scene of 307 lines the last act of <u>The Merchant</u> is the second-shortest. Rings play a part in the final discoveries: Julia in boy's clothes is discovered to be Julia when she shows the ring Proteus had given her, and Portia in her own attire is shown to have been the attorney when she displays the ring Bassanio had given her. Since Proteus repents and Valentine forgives, the friendship is preserved, and the two pairs of lovers marry. Since Antonio has been saved and Portia and Nerissa forgive, the friendship is preserved, and the two pairs of lovers are able to consummate their marriage.

Although it is generally believed that Shakespeare wrote his <u>Sonnets</u> before or at roughly the same time as <u>The Merchant</u>, and although they, like the drama, portray a more mature man caring very much for a younger man, the play echoes the poems only occasionally and at a distance. If Antonio's sadness in the opening scene is related to Bassanio's departure, it is similar to the poet's in Sonnets 40-42 (though the latter is referring to the young man's taking <u>his</u> lady): "Take all my loves, my love, yea, take them all, / . . . All mine was thine, before thou hadst this more" (40.1,4) and "That she hath thee is of my wailing chief, / A loss in love that touches me more nearly" (42.3-4). Sonnet 42 concludes with the conceit that "my friend and I are one" in loving the same woman, as Portia passes the ring through Antonio to Bassanio at the end of <u>The Merchant</u>.

In Sonnets 71-74 the poet, like Antonio in Acts 3 and 4, presents himself as approaching death and is unwilling to impose on the young man or put the

latter's future welfare in jeopardy. Sonnets 71-74
begin, "No longer mourn for me when I am dead"; "O,
lest the world should task you to recite"; "That time
of year thou mayst in me behold"; and "But be contented
when that fell arrest." In the last the poet imagines
himself arrested by death and refused bail, but the
young man should "be contented" because he retains the
poet's spirit, which is preserved in the poem. The
conceit that poetry preserves life beyond life has no
place in The Merchant; otherwise, there are similar
sentiments in the play:

> all debts are clear'd between you and I, if I
> might but see you at my death. Notwithstand-
> ing, use your pleasure; if your love do not
> persuade you to come, let not my letter.
> (3.2.318-22)

> [Slubber] not business for my sake, Bassanio,
> But stay the very riping of the time;
> And for the Jew's bond which he hath of me,
> Let it not enter in your mind of love.
> (2.8.39-42)

> Commend me to your honorable wife,
> Tell her the process of Antonio's end,
> Say how I lov'd you, speak me fair in death;
> And when the tale is told, bid her be judge
> Whether Bassanio had not once a love.
> (4.1.273-7).

The last passage comes as close as The Merchant can to
the idea of words preserving a life beyond life.

Usury is an occasional metaphor in The Sonnets,
most strikingly in 134, where the poet asks the dark
lady to restore the young man to him:

But thou wilt not [restore him], nor he will
                                not be free,
For thou art covetous, and he is kind;
He learn'd but surety-like to write for me
Under that bond that him as fast doth bind.
The statute of thy beauty thou wilt take,
Thou usurer, that put'st forth all to use,
<u>And sue a friend came debtor for my sake</u>,
                           [emphasis added]
So him I lose through my unkind abuse.

Like the usurer, the lady holds both the poet and the young man (who met and became attracted to her through the poet) in debt to her beauty and under the law of beauty refuses to let either of them be free. In the couplet the poet reflects on the triple irony that he has lost the young man to the lady, that the young man pays the whole debt, and that the poet still is not free:

Him have I lost, thou hast both him and me,
He pays the whole, and yet I am not free.

The roles are reversed in <u>The Merchant</u>, where the older man comes debtor for the young man's sake, and the latter feels obligated to offer life, wife, "and all the world" (4.1.284) for his older friend. Usury and the usurer (real or metaphorical) are the enemies of friendship in both <u>The Sonnets</u> and <u>The Merchant</u>. Usury is also a metaphor in Sonnets 4 and 6, bonds in Sonnets 87 and 142.

Sonnets appear in several of Shakespeare's plays: <u>Love's Labor's Lost</u>, <u>Romeo and Juliet</u>, <u>All's Well That Ends Well</u>, and (in abbreviated form) <u>The Two Gentlemen</u> and <u>A Midsummer Night's Dream</u>. There are none in <u>The Merchant</u>, but Bassanio's initial description of

Portia--a most appropriate occasion for a sonnet--is structured as an unrhymed sonnet:

> In Belmont is a lady richly left,
> And she is fair and, fairer than that word,
> Of wondrous virtues. Sometimes from her eyes
> I did receive fair speechless messages.
> Her name is Portia, nothing undervalu'd
> To Cato's daughter, Brutus' Portia.
> Nor is the wide world ignorant of her worth,
> For the four winds blow in from every coast
> Renowned suitors, and her sunny locks
> Hang on her temples like a golden fleece,
> Which makes her seat of Belmont Colchis' strond,
> And many Jasons come in quest of her.
> O my Antonio, had I but the means
> To hold a rival place with one of them,
> I have a mind presages me such thrift
> That I should questionless be fortunate!
>
> (1.1.161-76).

The thought and sentence structure of the Shakespearean sonnet typically support the rhyme scheme (ABABCDCDEFEFGG) in producing three quatrains and a couplet, but sometimes the thought and/or the sentence structure combine two quatrains into an octave. In Bassanio's speech a quatrain sentence tells us that the lady is rich, beautiful, virtuous, and loving. Then an octave sentence associates her with Brutus' Portia and the golden fleece. The final quatrain (instead of the sonnet's couplet) applies the ideas of the rest of the sonnet to the present situation as many of Shakespeare's concluding couplets do. Although he eschewed rhyme, a sonnet writer composed Bassanio's speech.

Chapter IV
The Develpment of the Characters (Except Shylock)

The last two chapters have emphasized Shakespeare's debt to various sources. On the other hand, the present chapter focuses both on the characters the dramatist added, and on his development of the characters he borrowed outside the framework of his source material as the play grew toward the shape we read or see in the theater. Since the genesis of Shylock--both the "sources" and the development of the character--are largely independent of Shakespeare's handling of the friends, lovers, and companions, this chapter, like its predecessors, will have little to say about him.

The flesh-bond story combined with the casket story required only four characters: the lady, the lover, the borrower, and the usurer. Other stories suggested a daughter for the usurer, and Shakespeare's practice as well as the personnel of his acting company postulated a clown. Effective use of the casket plot called for two unsuccessful suitors. In addition, for each of the four necessary characters, Shakespeare provided a confidant to create an excuse for dialogue, to provide variety and light contrast, to fill the stage with additional persons, to give a sense of wider world, to employ his fellow-actors, and to accomplish other purposes.

For Portia, the playwright created a "waiting woman," Nerissa, who is on stage with her mistress in every one of the nine scenes in which Portia appears. Nerissa, too, is never on stage alone: the ladies chaperone each other. <u>Nericcia</u> in Italian means "blackish" (i.e. "black-haired"), and Nerissa is a visual contrast to her mistress, who is blonde ("her sunny locks / Hang on her temples like a golden fleece," 1.1.169-70). Although Nerissa's presence might have been suggested by the maid in <u>Il Pecorone</u>, who betrays her mistress and is married to Ansaldo, or by Julia's maid Lucetta in <u>The Two Gentlemen</u>, who discusses the lady's suitors, or by the presence of <u>two</u> ladies who disguise themselves for the trial scene in <u>Zelauto</u>, the demands of the play itself would have been enough to create her. Without Nerissa, <u>The Merchant</u> would have only two female roles, fewer than any of Shakespeare's other comedies or his histories and romances. <u>The Two Gentlemen</u> also has three women's parts. Nerissa adds spirit to the play, mimics her mistress decorously (her marriage, also, depends on Bassanio's choice of caskets), and marries another of the confidants, Gratiano.

As his bride is always on stage with Portia, Gratiano usually appears with Bassanio, although not in 1.3, where his levity and the anti-Semitism he reveals in Act 4 would distract from the serious business of making the bond. However, Shakespeare makes use of him in 2.4 and 6 as part of the group of young men who help Lorenzo and Jessica elope. In contrast to the serious, decorous Bassanio, he is light-hearted and talkative,

also witty and bawdy (e.g., 5.1.237-38, 300ff.). In
behavior and contrast with the principal lover, he
resembles Mercutio in Romeo and Juliet. He also has
the function of railing at Shylock during the courtroom
scene and preferring that the Jew be hanged rather than
christened (4.1.133-38, 367, 398-400); his attitude
sets off the "mercy" of the other Christians while, no
doubt, expressing the harsh opinions of some of
Shakespeare's original audience. Graziano is the name
of a type character in the commedia dell'arte, the
doctor of law or medicine, who is usually in conflict
with the character called Pantalone. Gratiano uses
medical terminology at the beginning of his first long
speech (1.1.80-86), and, as we shall see, Shylock has
some of the characteristics of Pantalone. Typically,
Graziano is elderly, is presumptuous, and talks to
excess. As Bassanio's companion and an acceptable
lover, Gratiano cannot have the first characteristic,
but he has an abundance of the other two. John Florio
defines Gratiano as "a gull, a foole or clownish
fellowe in a play or comedie." Sometimes Graziano is
cuckolded, as Gratiano fears he is in Act 5.[1]

Salerio and Solanio are usually attached to
Antonio: with him they introduce the play, emphasizing
his wealth and the commercial world of Venice. Like
Gratiano, they have nothing to do with the making of
the bond (1.3), and also like him they participate in
Jessica's elopement (2.4 and 6). In 2.8 they describe
the parting of Bassanio and Antonio; they comment on
the loss of some of Antonio's ships; and they gloat
over Shylock's rage at losing his daughter and his
ducats—yet they fear that Antonio might have to "pay
for this" (26). In 3.1 they lament more losses for
Antonio before confronting Shylock, taunting him about

the loss of his daughter, and provoking his powerful speech on revenge. Through 3.1 their names have not been used in the speeches; presumably Shakespeare was willing that they should be anonymous Venetian gentlemen to the Elizabethan audience, who lacked a program. After Bassanio has chosen the correct casket, Salerio brings the news of Antonio's arrest from Venice, and the name Salerio is used five times in the speeches in 48 lines (3.2.219-66). Solanio (again unnamed in the dialogue) accompanies Antonio as prisoner in 3.3, and Salerio (also unnamed in the speeches) introduces Portia and Nerissa in disguise in the courtroom scene (4.1.107ff.). Thus, they are normally associated with Antonio and his affairs, though they also perform the functions of commentators, provocateurs, messenger, and doorman.

Their names are badly confused in the stage directions and speech prefixes of Q1: the stage directions describe them as Salaryno, Salanio, Salarino, Solanio, Salerino, and Salerio. The speech prefixes are inconsistent within scenes: in 1.1, for example, the stage direction's Salaryno and Salanio are abbreviated to Sola (which fits neither) and to Sala or Sal (which fits either). Scholars and editors have sometimes thought that three characters were involved, but in 1926 J. Dover Wilson demonstrated that there were only two--Salerio and Solanio.[2] He maintained that scribes and compositors were responsible for the confusion. With minor variations editors have generally followed his lead.

More recently (1975), Christopher P. Baker has pointed out that salario (Italian for "salary") was defined by Florio in his Worlde of Wordes as "a salarie, wages, hire, stipend, pension or pay given to

<u>servants</u>."[3]   Baker thinks the word appropriate as a
name, since their purpose is "to keep us informed about
the material wealth of Antonio and about Shylock's
concern for his ducats."   As Baker points out, the
forms of the names may be seen as variants of the
Italian <u>salario</u>--<u>Solanio</u> and <u>Salerio</u> being almost
indistinguishable in English pronunciation for <u>Salanio</u>
and <u>Salario</u>.

In the following year (1976) Yasumasa Okamoto
argued cogently that Wilson was "right in his
conclusions but wrong in his premises."[4]   Even though
his conclusions were accepted, Wilson's theory had not
fully satisfied scholars who thought the manuscript
from which Q1 was printed may have been Shakespeare's
own, in which case no scribe was involved.   Pointing
out that the playwright did not need to settle on the
names until 3.2 (and then on only one), Okamoto
suggested that Shakespeare began with <u>Salarino</u> and
<u>Salanio</u>, changed the latter to <u>Solanio</u> because the
abbreviations were confusing, and shortened the former
to <u>Salerio</u> with the accent on the second syllable as
more convenient metrically when he came to use it in
pentameter verse. (<u>Salerio</u> is also more flexible than
<u>Salarino</u> in that it can be trisyllabic or--as in
3.2.219--quadrisyllabic.) As Okamoto remarks, if this
theory is correct, it provides an interesting insight
into Shakespeare's way of writing and increases the
likelihood that the manuscript behind Q1 was
Shakespeare's autograph. Thus, there appear to be two
characters whose names, like their words, emphasize the
money side of Antonio and the money theme in <u>The</u>
<u>Merchant</u>.

The remaining confidant is Tubal.   Shylock is
normally isolated in the scenes in which he appears--

the Jew among Christians--and usually he keeps his own council.   In 1.3.41-52 Shakespeare gives him an extended aside on Antonio, and in 2.5.46-51 he confides in Jessica (or says in another aside) that he is glad to have the "Drone" Launcelot help Bassanio "to waste / His borrowed purse." But in 3.1 Shylock converses with his fellow-Jew Tubal, revealing through dialogue his efforts to find his daughter and his jewels, his agony over the cost of doing so, and the loss of the turquoise his wife Leah had given him--all in the context of his growing glee over Antonio's losses. The same information could have been conveyed more economically in soliloquy, but it emerges dramatically in conversation with Tubal, who, if not noticeably sympathetic, is at least not Shylock's enemy. Tubal's presence also suggests the Venetian community of Jews in the background, as does the rendezvous at the synagogue that Shylock arranges when he and Tubal part. Shylock's confidant does not appear again, but in the next scene (3.2.285) Jessica refers to her father's "countrymen" Tubal and Chus; since both names appear in Genesis 10, that may well be Shakespeare's source for the Hebrew names.

In addition to the four principal persons and their five confidants, there are nine named characters in the play.   Three--Leonardo, Balthazar, and Stephano--are functional servants. The other six may be conveniently discussed in pairs: Morocco and Arragon, Launcelot and Old Gobbo, and Lorenzo and Jessica.

Full theatrical use of the casket story demanded that the caskets be shown more than once, that suspense be raised for earlier choices before Bassanio's, and that the audience be fully cognizant of the inscriptions with their implications while knowing through the earlier failures which is the right casket so that in 3.2 they can concentrate on Portia and Bassanio as the latter chooses. Furthermore, the dramatized efforts of two striking characters' attempts to win the lady--one the proud victor in love and war and the other the extravagantly arrogant Spaniard-- enhance Portia's desirability, substantiating Bassanio's boast that "the four winds blow in from every coast / Renowned suitors" (1.1.168-69). As an African who is, by his own account, a famous personage in his world, Morocco helps justify both "Renowned" and "every coast." In 1.2 Nerissa lists and Portia comments on suitors from Naples, the Palatine, France, England, Scotland, and Saxony. To an Elizabethan it must have seemed odd that England's greatest enemy, the wealthiest and most powerful country in Europe, was unrepresented. The Prince of Arragon, bearing the name of one of the kingdoms of Spain and one of the leading Spanish families, suggesting a pun on "arrogant," and losing the lady through that allegedly most Spanish characteristic, pride, fills the gap nicely.

On his first appearance (2.1) Morocco is described by the stage direction as "a tawny Moor, all in white" (i.e., clad in white). There has been debate about whether tawny here means black or merely dark, whether Morocco is a Blackamoor or an Arab. Shakespeare may use tawny in the sense of black in Titus Andronicus 5.1.27 (the baby being described is "coal-black" five lines later), but elsewhere he uses it to mean "yellowish-brown."[5] The Oxford English Dictionary does not acknowledge "black" as a meaning for the word. Eldred Jones cites examples of Elizabethan usage to show that the term meant a "white" Moor (that is, an

Arab) as distinguished from a "black" Moor, and he thinks it is so used here.[6] In any case, the Prince's dark color contrasts with his white costume. His distinctive appearance combines with an heroic manner of speaking, his great deeds, his African origin, and (presumably) a different religion to create an impressive and exotic figure.

In 2.7 Morocco chooses the gold casket, which promises "what many men desire." He rejects the lead, for which he "must give and hazard all he hath" because it threatens without hinting at a reward and because his "golden mind stoops not to shows of dross." The silver casket, which promises "as much as he deserves" would be acceptable, because he thinks himself deserving in every way. But since gold is worth "ten times" as much as silver and because Portia's extraordinary desirability is shown by the suitors who come "from the four corners of the earth," he chooses, not unreasonably, "what many men desire." His reward is a skull and a scroll that tells him harshly that "All that glisters is not gold" and that his boldness is greater than his wisdom. However, he departs meekly, "A gentle riddance," Portia says.

In 2.9 Arragon is treated more harshly. He rejects the lead casket on much the same grounds as Morocco: "You shall look fairer ere I give or hazard." And he rejects the gold casket (the right decision) because he "will not jump with common spirits / And rank me with the barbarous multitudes" (the wrong reason, lacking humility). At some length he lectures on not receiving honors above one's merits--and then chooses to receive what he deserves: "I will assume desert." His reward is the portrait of a blinking idiot and a schedule that criticizes him for choosing "shadows," what was only "Silver'd o'er." He complains that he deserved more than a fool's head and is told by Portia that nobody can be judge of himself. He departs, observing bitterly that he came with one fool's head and leaves with two.

Arragon is treated more harshly than Morocco because he is the hated Spaniard and because, whereas Morocco's pride seems based on his actual exploits, Arragon's depends merely on his opinion of himself. Morocco is admirable, even if he is not a suitable husband for Portia, but Arragon is not. Both are treated unsympathetically in part because they are the rival lovers whose defeat gives us joy, as it does Portia and Nerissa. Also, as suggested earlier, many in Shakespeare's audience probably would have known the caskets story in Robinson's Gesta, where the choice is in religious terms and therefore absolute: choose God (the lead vessel) and receive Heaven; choose the world (gold or silver vessel) and receive Hell; there is nothing between.

In addition to evoking memories of Launce in The Two Gentlemen, Launcelot provides laughing comedy and fills the clown role that is traditional in Shakespeare's comic plays. Both the flesh-bond and the casket plots are deficient in laughter compared with the main plots of the previous comedies, The Comedy of Errors, The Taming of the Shrew, The Two Gentlemen, Love's Labor's Lost, and A Midsummer Night's Dream. In addition to the upstairs amusement that these plays offer, each has at least one clownish character of the servant or tradesman class. Launcelot has two scenes: 2.2, which begins with a 32-line soliloquy and continues through a dialogue with his father and a comic passage with Bassanio; and 3.5, an exchange with

Jessica and Lorenzo in Belmont. The soliloquy presents the Jew in a comic context as "a kind of devil" (24) and "the very devil incarnation" (27-28) to be fled from even if doing so means following the advice of the Devil himself. Since Jessica and Antonio, like Launcelot, also flee or escape from the Jew, the speech is a distorted mirror of action elsewhere in the play.

The passage with Old Gobbo probably develops from Launce's soliloquy in The Two Gentlemen, 2.3.14-26, where the clown addresses his shoe as his father and asks for its blessing. Launcelot toys with his blind father before kneeling down for his blessing before the old man, who feels his hair instead of his face and does not recognize him. This episode seems to be a comic parody of Genesis 27, where Jacob obtains the blessing of his blind father Isaac, who thinks he recognizes the hair of Esau. It continues the play's allusions to the Jacob story that Shylock initiated about 220 lines earlier when he told the story of Jacob and Laban and debated its meaning with Antonio. In passing, the Jew refers to the story of Isaac's blessing (1.3.73). Later, Shylock will swear "By Jacob's staff" (2.5.36) in Launcelot's presence, and in 3.1.121 he will reveal that his wife's name was Leah, which was also the name of Jacob's first wife. Below I will suggest that Shylock thinks of himself as following Jacob's example. In any event, in the scene with his father Launcelot is used to augment and reflect comically the Old Testament associations of the play.[7]

This function continues in 3.5, where Launcelot banters with Jessica over whether or not she is damned as "the Jew's daughter" (10-11), to which she replies that she is saved by her husband, who has made her a

Christian. Thus, the theme of escape from Shylock as escape from the Devil is revived, and the idea of conversion to Christianity, which will be forced upon Shylock in the next act, is introduced. The short passage that follows about Launcelot's having gotten the Moor pregnant provides, however briefly, the downstairs romantic entanglement that is common in Shakespeare's romantic comedies.

According to Q1 Launcelot tells us six times in the first nine lines he speaks that his name is Launcelet Iobbe. Iobbe is a form of Job, and the Third and Fourth Folios as well as Rowe's edition of 1709 printed Iobbe as Job. All editors since have followed dutifully Alexander Pope's emendation to Gobbo (1725), though some (e.g., Wilson and Brown)[8] acknowledge that it may be Job. There is no cast of characters in Q1, and the name Gobbo is never spoken on the stage by anyone. It comes from the stage direction at the end of Launcelot's soliloquy, where "old Gobbo" enters, and his speech prefixes through the rest of the scene are Gobbo and Gob. Gobbo means "hump-back" and was so defined by Florio; it was also a common family name in Italy.[9] Presumably, it describes Launcelot's father, who is often played as hunchbacked, but it has no clear reference to Launcelot, and, lacking programs and previous knowledge of the text, Shakespeare's audience would never know of it. No doubt it is possible that the playwright changed his mind between line 9 and the stage direction after line 32 or that somebody (perhaps a compositor) misread Gobbo as Iobbe six times but saw it to be Gobbo thereafter; yet neither possibility seems sufficient reason to emend the six instances in the speech to fit the silent name of another character. Even if Iobbe should be thought of as Launcelot's

absurdly idiosyncratic variation on Gobbo, the text
should still read Iobbe.

Another reason for preferring Iobbe is that we
might expect a word repeated frequently in the clown's
opening lines to be a joke. Launcelot not only recalls
the name of the clown in The Two Gentlemen, but it is
also a ridiculously pretentious name evoking memories
of Arthurian legend for a foolish character. There is
no apparent reason why Shakespeare should give
Launcelot a second proper name--no other character has
one--unless it adds to the comedy. Whereas Job was a
Jew known for his patience and suffering, Launcelot is
nervous and impatient; he is only comically long-
suffering under his master; and a Jewish name is
ridiculous for someone intent on escaping from the Jew.
Perhaps an affected Iobbe was delivered comically by
Will Kempe. In any case, Iobbe is a better joke as
applied to Launcelot than Gobbo, which is hardly a joke
at all.

As we have seen, Jessica may have been suggested
by Marlowe's Jew of Malta, Munday's Zelauto, Masuccio's
Il Novellino, a number of other sources, or simply the
playwright's desire for another pair of lovers and
another female role in the play. Many readers have
thought ill of Jessica. She is accused of deceiving
and stealing from her father (though she has no
alternative to deceiving him, and the ducats and jewels
may be regarded as her dowry), of spending extravagantly in Genoa (from the point of view of Tubal and
Shylock, who are hardly sympathetic with honeymooners),
and of betraying her father when she tells Portia and
Bassanio that she has overheard Shylock tell Tubal and
Chus that he preferred Antonio's flesh to his money
(3.2.284-90). Presumably pleasing her husband and his

friends, including saving the life of one of them, is more important to her than withholding information about her father's intentions--especially when doing so might encourage Portia and Bassanio not to take the threat seriously. As Warren D. Smith says,

> The Christians in Venice treat Jessica as an
> equal, and Portia and Nerissa in Belmont
> welcome her as a sister. The dramatist gives
> her a beautiful poetic scene with Lorenzo to
> open the final act, and she is treated as one
> of three heroines at the end of the play.[10]

Thus, it seems unlikely that Shakespeare expected his audience to think ill of Jessica, even though her name may be derived from Iscah, meaning "spy, or looker out."[11] The name is appropriate in that Shylock tells her to lock his doors and not "thrust [her] head into the public street / To gaze on Christian fools with varnish'd faces" (2.5.32-33). Her disobedience is part of her main action in the play. The dramatist may have found the name in Genesis 11.29, the next chapter after his probable source for Tubal and Chus--and Shylock.

In addition to being the Christian mate for the Jew's daughter, Lorenzo helps fill out the world of lively young men in Venice who surround Bassanio and Antonio. At the beginning of the final act he speaks the lovely duet with his wife, reintroducing the theme of love and beauty that he, Jessica, and Salerio had interrupted in 3.2 when they brought the bad news from Venice. Then he is the mouthpiece for two speeches on the value of music (5.1.49-88) that develop further the mood of beauty, harmony, and order while dissolving the harsh disharmony of the courtroom scene. Because of the passages in Act 5, Lorenzo's is the fifth-largest role in the play--at 180 lines, two lines longer than Gratiano's and Launcelot's--[12] yet to a reader he is less distinct as a person than they: he seems more functional than real. It is left to the actor to give him presence on the stage.

Of the four main characters, the one who has by far the largest role is Portia: she speaks 578 lines to Shylock's 361, Bassanio's 339, and Antonio's 188.[13] She appears in nine scenes to Shylock's five, is introduced before him, and leaves the stage more than three hundred lines after him. She dominates--often literally presides over--every scene in which she appears. Shylock dominates, too--except when he encounters her.

Shakespeare avoids scenes in which Portia might not obviously dominate or preside. There is no private love scene between the two principal lovers, where she would have had an equal. Although Portia and Bassanio express their love in 3.2, they do so in the presence of Gratiano, Nerissa, "and all their Trains" (i.e., Bassanio's and Portia's). Portia directs the scene as she did with Morocco and Arragon:

> Nerissa and the rest, stand all aloof.
> Let music sound while he doth make his choice;
> > (3.2.42-43).

When news comes of Antonio's arrest, she tells Bassanio what to do: marry her in church, take 60,000 ducats ("To pay the pretty debt twenty times over"), hurry to Venice, and bring his friend home--all without waiting to consummate the marriage. When we next see her (3.4), she is appointing Lorenzo to manage her house, sending Balthazar to Padua, and joking with Nerissa about her plans for Venice. In the courtroom scene the

Duke presides and Shylock dominates until Portia enters; she replaces both immediately. Finally, she dominates and presides in Act 5 at her own house. Earlier, with Morocco and Arragon, she welcomes the foreign princes graciously but firmly ("You must take your chance," 2.1.38) and dismisses them calmly, though presumably either of them might with uncharacteristic insight have chosen rightly./

Portia has been accused of breaking her obligation to her father's will by unconsciously or consciously hinting to Bassanio that he should choose the lead casket.[14] (Alternatively, it has been suggested that Nerissa, like the servant in Il Pecorone, gives the hint.) The song her musicians play and sing emphasizes that "fancy" (foolish love) is "engend'red in the eyes" and dies in its cradle, which can be understood as suggesting to Bassanio that he look deeper and not be misled by superficial appearances:

A song, the whilst Bassanio comments on the
caskets to himself.

Tell me where is fancy bred,
Or in the heart or in the head?
How begot, how nourished?
[All.] Reply, reply.
It is engend'red in the [eyes],
With gazing fed, and fancy dies
In the cradle where it lies.
Let us all ring fancy's knell.
I'll begin it. Ding, dong, bell.
All. Ding, dong, bell. (3.2.63-72)

The ingenuity of commentators has discovered that the first three lines rhyme with lead and that the last three lines rhyme with the letter L, which is the first

letter of lead. Bassanio seems to take the "hint,"
saying immediately after the song is finished, "So may
the outward shows be least themselves" and proceeding
to choose the lead casket.   Unfairly, it is said,
Morocco and Arragon are not given the benefit of the
song.   But surely it would be bad dramaturgy to have
the same song sung three times in the play. From the
point of view of the romantic story, Bassanio's is the
important choice, appropriately given emphasis not
provided for the others.

     There are two good reasons for supposing that
Shakespeare did not intend us to think that Portia
hints.   First, if she does hint, Shakespeare has
pointedly made her a liar. Earlier in this same scene
she has said,

> . . . I could teach you
> How to choose right, but then I am forsworn.
> So will I never be, so may you miss me,
> But if you do, you'll make me wish a sin,
> That I had been forsworn.   (3.2.10-14)

And in the speech immediately before the song, she
considers the possibility that Bassanio may lose:

> Then if he lose he makes a swan-like end,
> Fading in music. That the comparison
> May stand more proper, my eye shall be the stream
> And wat'ry death-bed for him.   (3.2.44-47)

Unless Shakespeare wished Portia to be a harshly
satiric portrait, it is hard to see why he would have
her make these emphatic statements at the romantic
climax of the play. Since Portia also says, "Nerissa
and the rest, stand all aloof," it seems that she may
be preventing her waiting woman from helping, too.

Second, Shakespeare has everything to gain for Bassanio's character by having him make the right choice without assistance. In the _Gesta_ the choice is made to prove the worthiness of the chooser. That was certainly the intent of Portia's father. Bassanio has no other action in the play that enables him to show courage or wisdom. He has compared the suitors of Portia to Jason (1.1.170-72), and just before he chooses Portia compares him with Hercules heroically rescuing Hesione from the sea monster:

> . . . Now he goes,
> With no less presence, but with much more love,
> Than young Alcides, when he did redeem
> The virgin tribute paid by howling Troy
> To the sea-monster. I stand for sacrifice;
> The rest aloof are the Dardanian wives,
> With bleared visages, come forth to view
> The issue of th' exploit. Go, Hercules,
> Live thou, I live; with much, much more dismay
> I view the fight than thou that mak'st the fray.
>
> (3.2.53-62)

This does not sound either like a lady who cheats or a playwright who intends her to cheat.

What, then, of the striking appropriateness of the song and Bassanio's apparent response to it? There are two answers. The first is provided by William Empson, who cites the song as an example of "a sort of dramatic ambiguity of judgment which does not consider the character as much as the audience." He continues,

> The audience is not really meant to think she
> is telling him the answer, but it is not
> posed as a moral problem, and seems a natural
> enough thing to do; she might quite well do

it in the belief that he would not hear; the
song is explaining to them [i.e., the
audience] the point about the lead casket,
may be taken to represent the fact that
Bassanio understands it, heightens the
tension by repeating the problem in another
form, and adds to their sense of fitness in
the third man being the lucky one.[15]

The song, then, may be seen as directed at the audience
rather than being a hint to Bassanio.

A second answer is that Bassanio is thinking about
the caskets and their inscriptions, and the song,
though sung by others, expresses what he is thinking.
Bassanio, not Portia or Nerissa, is expressing himself
in it. When Bassanio says, "So may the outward shows
be least themselves," he is continuing his own train of
thought represented by the words of the song rather
than suggested by them. The earlier part of his
thoughts is expressed in a different medium (song
rather than blank verse) to avoid repeating the
inscriptions, to emphasize the lyric and romantic mood,
and to provide variety. Such an interpretation is
consonant with the descriptive stage direction, "A
song, the whilst Bassanio comments on the caskets to
himself."

In choosing the name Portia for his heroine, the
dramatist was suggesting wealth, wisdom, and virtue.
As John Ruskin pointed out, Portia is "fortune lady"
(Latin portio = portion) as Perdita is "lost lady" and
Cordelia is "heart lady."[16] When Bassanio first
describes Portia, he tells Antonio, "Her name is
Portia, nothing undervalu'd / To Cato's daughter,
Brutus' Portia" (1.1.165-66). Named for the daughter
of the virtuous, wise philosopher and wife of the

virtuous republican, she is presented as a person of wisdom and virtue.

On the other hand, the connotations of the name Bassanio are elusive. It may have been suggested by the family of Italian musicians named Bassano (also Bassanie, Bassany, Bassanye) at the English court who were "conspicuously represented in the rosters of 'the King's Musick' (i.e., the establishment of instrumentalists and singers continuously attendant on the sovereign) over the whole period from 1540 to 1640."[17] The only connection of Shakespeare's Bassanio with music seems to be the song discussed above. A. L. Rowse has attempted to identify a member of the family, Emilia Bassanio Lanier, as the dark lady of Shakespeare's Sonnets.[18] There have also been efforts to associate Bassanio with bass and base, or with ordeals or touchstones (Greek basanoi).[19] Perhaps there was an allusion to the Bassano family, the point of which has been lost; the other associations do not seem convincing.

As we saw in Chapter II, the character and behavior of the young man in the pound-of-flesh story is usually weak. He is extravagant, lustful, greedy, and perhaps ambitious; he is foolish about the loan (or selfish if his friend borrows for him); he wins the lady by luck or with someone else's help; he does nothing to deserve the lady; and he is forgetful. The lady usually does not prefer him until he has managed to sleep with her. In contrast, Portia clearly cares for Bassanio from before the beginning of the play: "Sometimes from her eyes / I did receive fair speechless messages" (1.1.163-64), says Bassanio, and Portia remembers "well" the "Venetian, a scholar and a soldier, that came hither in company of the Marquis of

Monferrat." She remembers him as "worthy of [Nerissa's] praise" as "the best deserving a fair lady" (1.2.113-21).

The playwright's substitution of the challenge of the caskets for the challenge of staying awake lessens some of the problems. Bassanio is not presented as lustful, and--if we may assume he makes the choice among the caskets without help--he wins the lady through his wisdom, insight, and courage to take the "hazard" as well as good fortune; he has done something to deserve her. An analysis of his 35-line speech over the caskets (3.2.73-107) supports this view. He gives several examples to demonstrate that "outward shows" are "least themselves" and that "The world is still [i.e., always] deceiv'd with ornament." His examples come from law, religion, general morality, courage, and finally female beauty; and so he will not trust the "gaudy gold." Gold is what "many men desire," and his comments seem relevant. Although Arragon had made the same point, he had done so in a much more arrogant way. Equally, Bassanio will not choose the "pale and common drudge / 'Tween man and man," silver, perhaps alluding to the thirty pieces of silver paid to Judas. His comment fits the inscription on the casket ("as much as he deserves") in that as payment silver is "deserved." His lengthy comment on gold is to be taken as a rejection of silver as well: most people overestimate their deserts (silver) as well as other things (gold). He certainly avoids Arragon's mistake of thinking too highly of himself.

He chooses lead:

. . . But thou, thou meagre [poor, barren] lead
Which rather threaten'st than dost promise aught,
Thy paleness moves me more than eloquence,

And here choose I. Joy be the consequence!
(3.2.104-7)

Since his calling both silver and lead "pale" is
surprising, "paleness" has sometimes been emended to
"plainness." However, both silver and lead are indeed
"pale" beside "gaudy gold." Calling silver "pale" is
merely descriptive, whereas the lack of color in lead
reflects its meagerness and the inscription which
threatens rather than promises. "Eloquence" refers
both to the aggressive appearance of gold and the gaudy
promises of the first two inscriptions. Although he
refrains from saying so, the inscription on the lead
casket fits him: he is giving and hazarding all he has
and more.

The lover is traditionally extravagant and
forgetful. Shakespeare makes no effort to cover
Bassanio's extravagance, which is acknowledged in the
first scene. A young nobleman was expected to be
extravagant in late sixteenth-century England and to be
in debt; marrying a wealthy young lady and using her
money to pay the debts was a traditional way out.
Moreover, the play deliberately contrasts a free,
generous use of money with a selfish, destructive one.
Antonio lends his wealth freely without interest to
many and for friendship to one; Bassanio spends it
freely in pursuit of love; and Portia employs it
generously for her lover and his friend. Shylock, on
the other hand, lends money at interest, nearly undoes
many by it (Antonio says, "I oft deliver'd from his
forfeitures / Many that have at times made moan to me,"
3.3.22-23), makes it equal to his daughter's life, and
tries to kill Antonio with it. Both the mores of a
different age and the contrasts Shakespeare develops
within the play encourage an extravagant Bassanio.

Giannetto of Giovanni's <u>Il Pecorone</u> forgets his
godfather after he wins the Lady of Belmont, and some
of Bassanio's other predecessors also have faulty
memories. However, Shakespeare has Antonio's arrest
take place before Bassanio has chosen among the caskets
(the news reaches Belmont immediately after the
choice), thereby relieving him of ingratitude after his
success. Possibly Bassanio has waited too long to
choose, but at the beginning of 3.2 Portia urges him to
"pause a day or two / Before you hazard," implying that
he may have only recently arrived in Belmont.
Doubtless he, like the other characters, can hardly
believe that Shylock would really attempt to take the
pound of flesh, though he did protest briefly against
the bond when it was made: "You shall not seal to such
a bond for me, / I'll rather dwell in my necessity"
(1.3.154-55). The discovery appalls him moments after
his triumph over the caskets. It seems that
Shakespeare does about as much as he can with a
character who is somewhat "plot-ridden"--required to
act (or be inactive) in ways that cause difficulties
for a character who is expected to be both realistic
and attractive. Antonio and Portia both love him, and
Gratiano, Lorenzo, and the other young men admire him.
Shakespeare does not expect us to disagree.

The relative ages of Bassanio and Antonio are not
specified in <u>The Merchant</u>. Bassanio is unsettled in
life and seems younger than Antonio, who is an
established merchant worth the care and respect of the
Duke of Venice. Antonio's sadness at the beginning of
the play, his resignation when he is arrested (3.3),
and his passiveness in the courtroom scene suggest a
maturer, somewhat older man. In 1596-97, when <u>The
Merchant</u> was probably written, Shakespeare was thirty-

two or thirty-three. Among the wealthy, profligate
young men at court was his patron, Henry Wriothesley,
Earl of Southampton, to whom he had dedicated his Venus
and Adonis and Rape of Lucrece several years earlier;
born in October, 1573, he would have been about twenty-
three. Another was William Herbert, Earl of Pembroke,
to whom the First Folio would be dedicated by
Shakespeare's friends in 1623, born in 1580 and so
about seventeen at the time the play was written. Both
noblemen have been identified as the young man
addressed in Shakespeare's Sonnets. The playwright's
age seems not inappropriate for Antonio, and somewhere
between Pembroke's and Southampton's for Bassanio. One
would not be surprised to discover that the speaker of
The Sonnets, who expects to die some time before the
young man and who lies to the dark lady about his age
(Sonnet 138) was in his thirties and a dozen years,
more or less, older than the young man he urges to
marry in Sonnets 1-17.

Antonio, the Merchant of Venice, is the second of
six Antonios to appear in Shakespeare's plays. The
first is the father of Proteus in The Two Gentlemen,
the third the uncle of Hero in Much Ado about Nothing,
the fourth a sea captain and the loving friend of
Sebastian in Twelfth Night, the fifth the oldest son of
the Duke of Florence who walks across the stage in
All's Well That Ends Well (3.5.76) but speaks no lines,
and the sixth Prospero's wicked brother in The Tempest.
All except the minor example in All's Well are mature
men, and at least three are a generation older than the
lovers in their plays. With the notable exception of
Prospero's brother (and excluding the unknown character
in All's Well), they are good men. The sea captain who
befriends Sebastian and gives him his purse reminds one

most of the Venetian merchant and friend of Bassanio.
Probably The Two Gentlemen supplied the name for
Bassanio's friend as it supplied the name of the clown
in The Merchant, but thereafter Antonio seems to have
had pleasant connotations for Shakespeare. All this is
not to suggest that Antonio speaks for Shakespeare in
any definite way or that the playwright and his
creation held the same opinions on any particular
subject. Rather it seems probable that Shakespeare
found a story that encouraged him to develop a
character who may or may not be likable to others but
with whom the dramatist himself felt comfortably at
home.

In the first line of the play Antonio says that he
does not know why he is sad. His companions speculate
on reasons for the next seventy-five lines, and readers
have provided further explanations. Antonio denies
Salerio's suggestion that he is worried about his
argosies, Solanio's that he is in love, and Gratiano's
that he has "too much respect upon the world. / They
lose it that do buy it with much care" (1.1.74-75).
Readers have suggested that he suffers from the popular
Elizabethan disease, melancholia;[20] that he is unhappy
about Bassanio's forthcoming departure; that he has a
presentiment of disaster; that his sadness helps give
him an individual character; that it makes him careless
in signing the bond; and that it prepares for his
passiveness and resignation in the courtroom scene.
Although Antonio's companions may be mistaken, their
discussing the matter at such length makes it seem
important.

The readers' suggestions, which do not exclude
each other, are parts of the truth. If the plot calls
for too little action from Bassanio, it calls for even

less from Antonio. Once he has been brought to sign a bond for his own flesh--Shylock's idea--he has nothing more to do, and the more passive he is, the more the playwright can focus on Portia and Shylock. To give him the disease of melancholy, which inhibits action (common knowledge to all Elizabethans and all students of Hamlet) is at once to prepare for inactivity and to give Antonio a definite and fairly common, interesting characteristic. Left alone with Bassanio, he immediately asks about the "secret pilgrimage" to a lady "That you to-day promis'd to tell me of." Since he obviously knows that Bassanio will be leaving soon to pursue a life that will take him away from Antonio, it would be surprising if he were not responding with sorrow to Bassanio's departure.

Another reason for Antonio's sadness is that it sets off his eager enthusiasm to help Bassanio. As soon as the latter tells his friend that he needs help in obtaining money to pursue the lady, Antonio changes from a passive to an active, impatient mood:

> You know me well, and herein spend but time
> To wind about my love with circumstance,
>
> . . . .
>
> Then do but say to me what I should do
> That in your knowledge may by me be done,
> And I am prest unto it; therefore speak.
>
> (1.1.153-60)

After Bassanio has described Portia and his need for money, Antonio tells him, "Go presently [i.e., immediately] inquire, and so will I, / Where money is," and he will obtain it for Bassanio. Lethargic otherwise, he is pathetically eager to help his friend

depart, and so he is set up better than Shylock can
know to accept any terms for the loan.

Chapter V
The Selection and Arrangement of the Scenes

Chapter II included a discussion of Shakespeare's selection and arrangement of scenes in The Merchant, especially in Acts 1 and 2, in imitation of The Two Gentlemen. In this chapter the choice and sequence of scenes are studied in terms of their uses in the The Merchant--their relation to the plots, climaxes, characters, and themes of the play itself.

The playwright must decide which of many potential scenes to develop, which to ignore, and which to describe briefly by narration. An effective example of the last is 2.8, where in fifty-three lines Salerio and Solanio describe the parting of Antonio and Bassanio, Shylock's rage at his daughter's elopement, and the growing losses of Antonio. Each of these might have been the subject of a separate scene, and the last two would have helped prepare for the climax in the courtroom. Examples of other events and situations in the story that are not dramatized in the play include the actual signing of the bond, Shylock's coming home to find his daughter gone (a situation most effectively dramatized by Henry Irving in a silent addition to 2.6)[1], Jessica's extravagance in Genoa, Bassanio's being greeted by Portia on his arrival in Belmont, the previously mentioned private love scene between Bassanio and Portia (with a private exchange between Gratiano and Nerissa), the response of Dr. Bellario to the letter Portia sends to him by Balthazar (3.4.47-50), and Launcelot's affair with the Moorish woman. Except perhaps for the Dr. Bellario scene, all these could be effective in the theater; but they would not advance the plot or reveal anything new we need to know about the characters. For the most part, The Merchant is an economical play.

Except for its conclusion, the flesh-bond story itself is undramatic, and Shakespeare handles it with dispatch. Of twenty scenes in modern editions of The Merchant, only five are primarily concerned with the bond story. Two are fully developed--1.3, where the bond is proposed and accepted and which is lively because it introduces the character of Shylock and the conflict with Antonio that makes the bond seem plausible, and 4.1, where the story is resolved in the courtroom. With 457 lines, the latter is very fully developed. Between these two are three scenes in Act 3 that look toward the action in the courtroom. Scenes 1 and 3 bracket Bassanio's choice among the caskets, the first enabling Shylock to deliver his speech on revenge and reveal his deepening hatred in the conversation with Tubal, and the second (prepared for by the first) showing Shylock rejecting the pleas of Antonio, who is under arrest and resigned to the worst "To-morrow" (3.3.34) before the Duke. Next (3.4) we are shown Portia preparing for her trip to Venice. Thus, the two main participants and the intended victim are pointed toward the courtroom. The five scenes total 888 lines, more than half of which are spoken in the courtroom.

Little more than one third of the play is directly
concerned with the pound of flesh.

The caskets story is also developed in five
scenes, in somewhat more leisurely fashion considering
the substance of the story. It offers romance and
poetry, visual interest, striking characters in Morocco
and Arragon, and three moments of suspense. One scene
(1.2) is used to introduce Portia without advancing the
plot and another to present Morocco, again without
advancing the plot. Then alternate scenes (2.7, 2.9,
3.2) take us through the three possible choices and
Bassanio's triumph. Together, the bond and casket
stories occupy half the twenty scenes and about sixty
percent of the lines in the play.

The ring story is prepared for in 3.2.171-74 and
183-85 as Portia gives and Bassanio accepts the symbol
of their love. It begins with the last lines spoken in
the courtroom, is the subject of the brief scene that
follows (4.2), and is also the subject of most of the
last half of 5.1--a total of about 180 lines. The
elopement of the Jew's daughter occupies four short
scenes in Act 2 (3 through 6), a total of 185 lines.
It fills the time as Bassanio journeys to Belmont and
the bond matures. The two scenes in which Launcelot is
the main character (2.2, 3.5) total 296 lines. Both
give a sense of time passing, the first in conjunction
with 2.3-6 and the second between Portia's preparations
in Belmont and the courtroom scene.

Two scenes are not accounted for: 2.8, mentioned
previously, in which Salerio and Solanio summarize for
us briefly much that has happened, and the first scene
in the play. The latter introduces the title character
and friend, Antonio, and then the young man in love
with Portia. No mention is made either of Shylock or

of the caskets. Established emphatically at the beginning of the play, this friendship theme is referred to periodically thereafter (especially in 1.3.63-64; 2.8.36-42; 3.2.259-66, 292-302, 317-22; 3.3.35-36; 4.1.117-18, 275-87, 449-51; 5.1.249-53).

In arranging the scenes, Shakespeare alternates locales from Venice to Belmont, moving us from the former to the latter seven times. The scene divisions provided by Rowe and later editors conceal how regular the alternation is. Since the stage is cleared momentarily four times between Launcelot's soliloquy and Jessica's elopement, Pope (1723) divided the 391 lines of 2.2-6 into five scenes. However, all the action may be thought of as taking place in the street in front of Shylock's house, and the five scenes might be thought of as a single unit.[2] Again, at the end of 3.4 the stage is briefly empty as Portia departs for Venice before Launcelot and Jessica enter; but both scenes are in or near Portia's house and may also be thought of as a single unit. Finally, the nineteen lines of 4.2, with Gratiano catching up with Portia and Nerissa as they cross the stage, may be regarded as an extension of the courtroom scene. With these three adjustments--which convey the impression of the play, especially in the theater, even if they technically stretch the conventional definition of a scene--each "scene" in Venice is followed by one in Belmont and vice-versa with perfect regularity. About 55 percent of the lines are spoken in Venice and about 45 percent in Belmont. As many readers have noted, Shakespeare associates Venice with commerce, money-lending, hatred, conflict, and the rigid application of the law. Belmont ("beautiful mount") he associates with freedom from financial concerns, love, music, harmony, and

mercy within the order provided by law. The movement
of the play is from Venice to Belmont, where the
friends and lovers and clown assemble for the happy
ending.

Each of the acts into which the First Folio text
and all subsequent editions have been divided has a
climax: in Act 1 the climax is the agreement about the
bond; in Act 2 it is the successive failures of Morocco
and Arragon, who might have stolen Portia before
Bassanio's arrival; in Act 3 it is Bassanio's choice of
the correct casket; in Act 4 it is the defeat of
Shylock; and in Act 5 it is the reconciliation of
friends and lovers after the artificial quarrel over
the rings.

For much of the nineteenth century the last act of
The Merchant was omitted on the stage. In 1802 Richard
Valpy published his version of the play "As It Was
Acted at Reading School" with a substitute ending that
seems to have been followed in part by Charles Kean,
Edwin Booth, and others. For a time, French's acting
edition printed Valpy's ending. Henry Irving, too,
sometimes ended the play with Act 4.[3] Valpy moved the
opening passages of Act 5 (the duet of Lorenzo and
Jessica with the former's lines on music) to the
beginning of 3.4. He also added a new 30-line passage
to the end of the courtroom scene, in which Portia
throws off her doctor's gown and gives Antonio the good
news that three of his argosies are safe. There is no
ring story with this ending. In explanation, Valpy
declared that Shakespeare's fifth act was anti-
climactic after the interest of the courtroom scene.
Although Valpy may be right that the fifth act is an
anti-climax, its purposes are to return the play to the
friends and lovers in mood as well as in action and to

conclude the play as a comedy. Consequently, we are
treated in rapid succession to a duet about famous
lovers, a comic farewell from Launcelot, music and
philosophical comment on music, and light reflections
from Portia before the husbands are comically tormented
and forgiven, Antonio's argosies are found, and Lorenzo
and Jessica receive the deed from "the rich Jew" (292)
that is to assure their future. This is one of only
two passing allusions to Shylock in Act 5.

Chapter VI
The Genesis of Shylock

It may seem surprising that one can discuss The Merchant at length with only occasional reference to Shylock. However, the Jew is in various respects separate from the rest of the play. Not only are the sources for the character largely outside the earlier versions of the flesh-bond story, but also there is little that anticipates him in Shakespeare's earlier works. Although Shylock is Antonio's enemy and his hatred and use of money for destructive purposes are contrasted with friendship, love, and the use of money unselfishly to support them, he is not so much the deliberate enemy of the Christians' values as indifferent to them: he does not try to destroy friendship, but only a particular person for his own reasons, and he has no designs on the lovers. As the necessary antagonist in the flesh-bond plot he touches the story in a very important but still a limited way. Also, Shylock is a more fully developed character from harshly realistic (as opposed to romantic) drama; he would be more at home in the world of Ben Jonson's Volpone than he is in the world of idealized friendship and a wealthy, beautiful fairy-tale princess who is protected by riddling caskets.

Discussions of Shylock have often focused on whether the main sources of his character are to be found among Jews and records of Jews in Elizabethan England, in the medieval theological idea of Jews, or (his Jewishness being less important) in Elizabethan attitudes toward usury and usurers. The disagreement involves different meanings for the word Jew. Considerable effort has been spent demonstrating that, despite the banishment of Jews three centuries earlier, there were a few "Jews" (persons of Hebrew descent who were at least recently practicers of the Jewish religion) living in Shakespeare's England. Other scholars have claimed that the few such people living in England would not have practiced their religion openly but would have at least pretended to be Christians, so that there were not really any "Jews" (persons actively and openly practicing the Jewish religion) in England. Therefore, it is said, Shakespeare and his audience must have relied on ideas from earlier times, namely the medieval theological idea of Jews (to be discussed below). Some have argued further that in the absence of true "Jews" practicing their religion openly, the word Jew was applied to hard-hearted, unscrupulous, usurious, Protestant (especially Puritan) money-lenders; that these persons meant much more to Elizabethans than ethnic or religious "Jews"; that usurers were common, conventional figures on the Elizabethan stage while Jews were not; and that therefore Shylock was much more significant as usurer than as "Jew" in either of the other senses of the word. As we have seen, the ballad

Gernutus draws a moral about usurers rather than about Jews.

Writing in 1879, Frederick W. Hawkins was apparently the first to associate Shylock with an historical Jew, Dr. Roderigo Lopez, the Portuguese Jew who was tried for treason in February 1594 and was executed at Tyburn four months later.[1] Pamphlets kept the case before the public, and probably as a result, Marlowe's Jew of Malta was revived in 1594-95 and again in 1596.[2] Lopez had settled in England by 1559; he had been baptized, and he professed to be an Anglican. He became physician to Secretary Walsingham and the Earls of Leicester and Essex; after 1586 he was chief physician to Queen Elizabeth. He was an advisor to Don Antonio, the Portuguese pretender, who was supported by Elizabeth and Essex; and Sidney Lee, who took up Hawkins' suggestion, thought Shakespeare might have met him through Essex's friend, the Earl of Southampton.[3] Lopez corresponded with King Philip of Spain, who apparently thought he was sympathetic to Spanish intentions, though in fact Lopez usually passed on what he learned from Spanish sources to Elizabeth's ministers. Eventually, however, he offended Essex, and when the Spanish tried to bribe him to poison the Queen, Essex accused him of treason. Lopez was at least threatened with the rack, was tried before Essex himself, and was found guilty. After delays and with much reluctance, the Queen finally allowed his execution. His alleged statement on the scaffold that "he loved the Queen as well as he loved Jesus Christ" was not well received by the large crowd at his execution.[4]

Lee noted references in The Merchant to the rack, the halter, the jurymen, and a hanged wolf (4.1.134, the Latin *lupus* for wolf allegedly reflecting the Elizabethan pronunciation of *Lopez*, sometimes spelled *Lopus*). Yet, though he entitled his article "The Original of Shylock," Lee concluded with the admission that he was "not presumptuous enough to imagine" that he had identified the "actual original of Shylock": the character, he thought, might have been based upon another Jew, perhaps one associated with Lopez. Other scholars have emphasized the possible effects of these events on Shakespeare's imagination, even if several years later.[5] Arguing further that Jews other than Lopez were present in sixteenth-century England despite the law against their presence, Lee cited a meeting to discuss Jews in England between Henry VII and the Spanish Ambassador at the time of Prince Arthur's marriage to Catherine of Aragon.[6] He found the names of a few Jews, and in 1928 Lucien Wolf discovered the existence of a community of Marranos (Jews who had adopted or pretended to adopt Christianity) in London, concluding that there were at least eighty or ninety Jews living in Elizabeth's England.[7] Later, Charles Sisson provided further details of Jews in London, including an account of a Chancery suit in 1596--about the time *The Merchant* was being written--by Mary May, the widow of an English merchant, against two Portuguese Jews who resided in London. In the course of the suit Mrs. May claimed that the Jews practiced their faith and that their religion interfered with their business services. Evidence was received on both points. After taking pains to be informed and objective, the Court agreed with the justice of Mrs. May's case but urged her to show compassion towards the Jews. Sisson considered the verdict "an eminently fair decision."[8]

Cecil Roth has pointed out that Elizabethan travelers' accounts of Italian ghettos were likely sources of information for Shakespeare.[9] Other scholars, including Cardozo and Warren D. Smith, have disagreed with Lee and Wolf, maintaining that since the few "Jews" in England would normally have been behaving like Christians, they are unlikely to have contributed significantly to the views held by playwrights or their audiences.[10] Both argue that the less likely Elizabethans were to encounter recognizable Jews in real life, the more important was the Christian theological view of Jews and its adaptation in literary works to the interpretation of Shylock. Smith summarizes succinctly this theological view:

> Such widely read literary works as the Cursor Mundi (composed about the time of the 1290 expulsion [and containing a version of the flesh-bond plot]), Chaucer's "Prioress's Tale," North's Diall of Princes, Lyly's Euphues, and Nashe's Unfortunate Traveler contain invectives against the Jews as the killers of Christ; and medieval drama, together with medieval art, linked the Jew with the devil. In the miracle plays Judas was on several occasions played as a bloody-minded usurer, and the morning-star of the Reformation, Martin Luther, preached several sermons against the Jews. . . . The Jew could be forgotten in post-expulsion England as an undesirable neighbor but never as the slayer of Jesus Christ.[11]

As the alleged crucifiers of the Son of God, servants of the devil, poisoners of wells in Christian

countries, and murderers of innocent children, Jews
seemed rightfully the objects of hatred and persecution. This attitude lies directly behind Launcelot's
soliloquy in 2.1 ("Certainly the Jew is the very devil
incarnation"), Gratiano's attitude toward Shylock in
the courtroom scene, and Shylock's own comment on
Antonio, "I hate him for he is a Christian" (1.3.42).

Other scholars have given indirect support to the
view that Shylock is based on the theological rather
than the real Jew by arguing that he is not an accurate
picture of a Jew, who would not have a non-Jewish
servant or leave his daughter alone in the house with
such a person; who would not "cut off a piece, even the
smallest portion of a living animal" or swear by
Jacob's staff, his tribe, or the Sabbath; who would
have been taught to show mercy; and whose case would
have been thrown out of a Talmudic court, which would
have punished him for bringing it.[12] Near the end of
his book written before he fled from Hitler's Germany,
Hermann Sinsheimer described Shylock as an unreal
figure representing a real argument--a myth with a
mission:

> The mythical transformation of the Jew
> through the medieval centuries and three
> centuries without any first-hand experience,
> gave the Elizabethans their picture of
> Jewishness, or what was left of it: a
> speaking image, a walking, talking and acting
> phantom, a legendary creature . . . [to whom]
> the poet could attribute the improbable and
> impossible, even the cutting of a pound of
> flesh from a live body in a court of
> justice. . . .

> The old fable yielded the material and
> the cause. But Shakespeare did the
> rest. . . . No Jewish "problem" is expressly
> touched. But in some way or other Shylock's
> arguments, reflecting the fate of the
> medieval and post-medieval Jew, make up for
> this. He becomes the spokesman of the
> bondsmen of medieval Christianity.[13]

Of course, this is a modern view. The average
Elizabethan may well have responded to the myth much
more and to the mission much less than a modern
audience.

To some, including Cardozo, Warren Smith, John W.
Draper, and Grebanier, the lack of real models for
Shakespeare's Jew leads to emphasizing Shylock's usury
at the expense of his Jewishness. Draper surely
overstates his case when he says, "Shylock the Jew was
merely Venetian local color; Shylock the usurer was a
commentary on London life."[14] More moderately, Brown
observes that "In contrast to the 'Jewish problem,' the
rights and wrongs of usury were a living issue to
Elizabethans."[15]

The arguments against "usury," a term which for
Elizabethans normally meant charging any interest at
all, had both Classical and Old Testament authority.
Aristotle had said that usury is unnatural; it

> is most reasonably hated, because its gain
> comes from money itself and not from that for
> the sake of which money was invented. For
> money was brought into existence for the
> purpose of exchange, but interest increases
> the amount of the money itself (and this is
> the actual origin of the Greek word [tokos

> meaning both "offspring" and "interest for
> money"]: offspring resembles parent, and
> interest is money born of money);
> consequently this form of the business of
> getting wealth is of all forms the most
> contrary to nature.[16]

There is an Elizabethan proverb that "an Usurer is one
that puts his money to the unnatural act of generation,
and the scrivener is his bawd"[17] (emphasis added). It
is to this way of thinking that Antonio refers when he
asks Shylock whether he thinks his gold and silver are
ewes and rams, and Shylock answers that he makes them
breed as fast (1.3.95-96). Deuteronomy 23.20 provided
the text, "Unto a stranger thou maiest lend upon
usurie, but thou shalt not lend upon usurie unto thy
brother."[18] The medieval church said that, since all
Christians are "brothers," they could not charge each
other interest.[19] As Thomas Wilson wrote in his
Discourse upon Usury (1572), "God ordeyned lending for
maintenaunce of amitye and declaration of love betwixt
man and man."[20] Or as Antonio puts it, "for when did
friendship take / A breed for barren metal of his
friend?" (1.3.133-34).

In the "Introduction" to his edition of Thomas
Wilson's work, R. H. Tawney outlines the history of the
controversy over the taking of interest during the
sixteenth century. Both conservatives and reformers
assumed that economic conduct was amenable to moral
criteria, but conservatives held that the relevant
moral criteria were expressed through canon law and
established state and municipal law (which forbade the
taking of interest, though it allowed a number of other
speculative practices). Reformers, on the other hand,
tried to reconcile theory with contemporary practice:

Luther argued that avoiding injury to one's neighbor
and following the law of Christian charity were the
important criteria, and Calvin rejected the notion that
money does not breed money on the basis that money is
not essentially different from land or other goods for
the use of which one expects to pay. In England the
Act of 1545 allowed the taking of interest at ten
percent, but in 1552 this provision was repealed, and
the taking of interest was forbidden on pain of fine,
imprisonment, and loss of interest and principal.
Based in part on a distinction between "usury" and
"true and fair interest," the compromise Act of 1571
provided that contracts of up to ten percent were
legal. Contracts of more than ten percent were
invalid, and Tawney understands the Act to say that
interest was not legally protected on contracts of ten
percent or less, since the borrower was permitted to
recover the interest in the courts if he was willing to
lose his reputation as a credit risk. However, Tawney
points out that the "doctrineless individualism" of the
merchant class was separating economics from ethics and
thereby turning the flanks of both groups of theorists:
"By the reign of James I [the merchants] had almost
come into their own."[21]

The point of view of the Elizabethan antagonist of
usury is articulated forcefully by Wilson in his
"Preface" addressed to the Earl of Leicester. He asks
the Earl to reform or take away "one especial mischiefe
as yll, nay woorse than anye plague":

> I do meane that ouglie, detestable and
> hurtefull synne of usurie, whiche, being but
> one in grossenes of name, caries many a
> mischief linked into it in nature, the same
> synne beinge nowe so rancke througout all

Englande, not in London onelye, that men have altogether forgotten free lending, and have geven themselvees wholye to lyve by fowle gayning, makinge the lone of monye a kinde of merchandise, a thinge directlye against all lawe, against nature, and against god. And what should this meane, that, in steade of charitable dealing, and the use of almose [alms] (for lending is a spice thereof), hardenes of harte hath nowe gotten place, and greedie gayne is cheefelye folowed, and horrible extorcion commonly used? I do verely beleve, the ende of thys worlde is nyghe at hande.[22]

Presumably not many of Wilson's persuasion went to the theater, but his attitude must have been present in milder form among many who did. Today the treatment of minorities is a living issue, whereas lending money at interest is generally accepted; for the Elizabethans, lending at interest was an important issue, while unfair treatment of minorities was generally overlooked.

As real-life usurers were much more common than Jews, so also stage-usurers were much more common than stage-Jews. Arthur B. Stonex studied more than sixty plays written between 1553 and 1643 (most of them after 1600) that include a money-lender and a borrower. He noted that the defeat of the money-lender evolved from the device of a crude _deus ex machina_ in morality plays "to two very popular _deae ex machina_ who flourished in numerous amusing and highly complicated comedies of the Elizabethan and Jacobean heyday"--the daughter who elopes with the father's prodigal debtor and the heiress who rejects the money-lender as a suitor and marries the prodigal debtor. Stonex observed that if Bassanio had eloped with Jessica or Shylock had been an unsuccessful suitor of Portia, one type or the other would have been fully developed in <u>The Merchant</u>.[23] Wright described the typical characteristics of the usurer in Elizabethan dramatic and non-dramatic literature: he is the old suitor of a young woman; he is loathsome and hideous, has a large nose, wears spectacles, has a cough, suffers from dropsy or gout resulting in ill-temper, never eats well except at the expense of a neighbor or debtor, ruins his betters, is hard on his servants, dresses badly, and dies in various ways, but "the orthodox writer will . . . prefer to assign the halter."[24] He sins against God by worshiping gold and shows his mistrust of God by storing up riches; he lives poorly and has a guilty conscience. He lacks heirs, or his heirs do not love him, or they are prodigals or fools.

Shylock eats at the expense of a debtor, tries to ruin his better, is hard on his servant, is wished a halter, is unduly interested in his ducats, and is unloved by his prodigal heir. He is often played with a large nose, but whether he wears spectacles, has a cough, and dresses badly depends on the performance; he may have had these characteristics on the Elizabethan stage. Shakespeare saves him from the indignities of being an absurd suitor, living very poorly, suffering from a bad conscience, and being hanged. He is clearly developed within the convention, yet he is a humanized, not a caricatured example of it.

Paul N. Siegel has developed the parallels between <u>Puritan</u> usurers in Elizabethan England and Shylock. Not only was it the Puritans who did most of the money-lending, but their enemies tended to characterize them as quoting the Old Testament, as being hypocritical (as Shylock is in eating with the Christians despite his professed scruples), and being arrogant. They disliked merry-making, were cruel, and were sometimes referred to as "devils."[25]

However, the word usurer is used only once in The Merchant and then by Shylock himself, who says of Antonio, "He was wont to call me usurer, let him look to his bond" (3.1.47-48). Shylock is offended by the term and feels that it adds to his legitimate grudge against the merchant. The word usury is not used in the play at all; Shylock employs usance (usances) three times, a word spoken by no other character in Shakespeare's plays. It is surprising that, insulting as the Christians sometimes are to or about Shylock, they never refer to him as usurer. Instead, for them he is Jew 61 times in the play. Another 30 times he is Jew in the stage directions and speech prefixes of Q1, probably the playwright's choice of terms. By contrast, the personal name Shylock is used by other characters only 15 times, but it appears on 57 occasions in the directions and prefixes. There are three related points of interest here: the meanings of the word Jew in Shakespeare's day, the characters' preference for Jew over both usurer and Shylock, and a pattern to be observed in the appearances of the generic and personal names in the directions and prefixes as a possible clue to the playwrights's attitude or intentions.

The Oxford English Dictionary has two definitions for the substantive Jew. The first is ethnic and religious:

A person of Hebrew race; an Israelite. . . . any Israelite who adhered to the worship of

Jehovah as conducted at Jerusalem. . . .
almost always connoting [Jews'] religious and
other characteristics, which distinguish them
from the people among whom they live, and
thus often opposed to <u>Christian</u>, and (esp. in
early use) expressing a more or less
opprobrious sense.

Examples are from c. 1275 on and include Shylock's
line, "I am a Jew. Hath not a Jew eyes?" (3.1.58-59).
The second definition is:

As a name of opprobrium or reprobation; <u>spec.</u>
applied to a grasping or extortionate money-
lender or usurer, or a trader who drives hard
bargains or deals craftily.

This definition says nothing about ethnic origins or
religious practices. It is represented in the <u>OED</u> by
only one example from before 1700: in George Chapman's
<u>Sir Giles Goosecap</u> (1601-03), "If the sun of thy beauty
do not white me like a [shepherd's] holland, I am a Jew
to my Creator."[26] Alan Dessen quotes a similar use of
the word from a letter Princess Elizabeth wrote to her
sister Queen Mary almost half a century earlier (1556):

When I revolve in mind (most noble Queen) the
old love of pagans to their princes, and the
reverent fear of the Romans to their senate,
I cannot but muse for my part, and blush for
theirs, to see the rebellious hearts and
devilish intents of Christians in name, but
Jews in deed, towards their anointed
King. . . .[27]

Both passages refer to the Jew as the type of the hard-
hearted traitor who would destroy Christ, the Son of

his Creator and the King of kings. Both elevate the comparatively tame, domestic definition of the OED to the level of high (if absurd) romance or high politics.

They are examples, about forty years before The Merchant was written and about five years after, of the word Jew used to imply a moral condition. G. K. Hunter cites Barabas' opening speech in The Jew of Malta as dramatizing the materialistic attitude implied by this sense of the word Jew. Barabas gloats over his riches:

> What more may heaven do for earthly man
> Than thus to pour out plenty in their laps,
> Ripping the bowels of the earth for them,
> Making the sea their servants, and the winds
> To drive their substance with successful blasts?[28]
>
> (1.1.105-9)

From the early seventeenth century he cites George Herbert's "Self-condemnation," in which he who chooses "This worlds delights before true Christian joy, / Hath made a Jewish choice" and

> He that hath made a sorrie wedding
> Between his soul and gold, and hath preferr'd
> False gain before the true,
> Hath done what he condemnes in reading:
> For he hath sold for money his deare Lord,
> And is a Judas-Jew.[29]

Hunter observes:

> The Elizabethan word 'Jew', in fact, like
> many other words which are nowadays taken in
> an exact racialist sense ('Moor' and 'Turk'
> are the obvious other examples), was a word
> of general abuse, whose sense, in so far as

it had one, was dependent on a theological
rather than an ethnographical framework.[30]

Shakespeare uses the word _Jew_ eight times in plays
other than _The Merchant_. In three instances he uses it
to mean a hard-hearted person, twice in _The Two_
Gentlemen and once in _Much Ado about Nothing_.[31] Both
examples from the first play are spoken by Launce, who
describes his dog Crab as indifferent to Launce's
parting with his family:

> I think Crab my dog be the sourest-natur'd
> dog that lives: my mother weeping, my father
> wailing, my sister crying, our maid howling,
> our cat wringing her hands, and all our house
> in a great perplexity, yet did not this
> cruel-hearted cur shed one tear. He is a
> stone, a very pibble-stone, and has no more
> pity in him than a dog. A Jew would have
> wept to see our parting. (2.3.5-12)

Two scenes later Launce scolds Speed for lack of
"charity" in not joining him at the alehouse: "thou art
an Hebrew, a Jew, and not worth the name of a
Christian" (2.5.54-57). Despite the references to
Hebrew and Christian, the second example says nothing
about Speed's ethnic origins or religious practices:
hard-heartedness is entirely the point. A few years
later, in _Much Ado_, Shakespeare has Benedick, feeling
that he must respond to Beatrice, say, "If I do not
take pity of her, I am a villain; if I do not love her,
I am a Jew" (2.3.262-63). Again there is no ethnic or
religious point.

In _The Merchant_ the word _Jew_ is not normally used
in the pure sense of hard-heartedness, if only because
Shylock is indeed an ethnic and religious Jew.

Sometimes the Christians add an opprobrious adjective, as in "the villain Jew." However, Antonio uses <u>Jewish</u> in the <u>OED</u>'s second sense in the courtroom:

> You may as well do any thing most hard
> As seek to soften that--than which what's
> > harder?--
> His Jewish heart!   (4.1.78-80)

Launcelot, too, is thinking of the Jew's hard heart when he says, "My master's a very Jew. Give him a present! give him a halter. I am famish'd in his service" (2.2.104-6). Two traditional associations with the usurer (the starved servant and the halter) are evoked here. The idea of hard-heartedness adds to Antonio's irony when, punning on <u>gentle</u> and <u>gentile</u>, he calls Shylock a "gentle Jew" and then adds to the paradox, "he grows kind" (1.3.177-78). Always able to carry at least the potential of the double meaning for Shakespeare and his audience, <u>Jew</u> serves the purpose of keeping the character's hard-heartedness before us almost as well as <u>usurer</u> might. It seems that Shakespeare wanted to employ the associations of the usurer but employ them lightly--or at any rate less than he could have done.

For the original texts of a Shakespeare play to use a generic term in the directions and prefixes alternately with a personal name (or even in lieu of it) is not uncommon: Launcelot is sometimes <u>Clown</u>, sometimes <u>Launcelet</u> or <u>Launce</u> in <u>The Merchant</u>, and Claudius is <u>King</u> in the Second Quarto of <u>Hamlet</u> except in one direction and one prefix. Yet there seems to be a pattern to the distribution of <u>Jew</u> and <u>Shylock</u> in this play. There is a rough correspondence between Shylock's most emphatic speeches either as religious

Jew or as heartless usurer and the generic prefix _Iew_, whereas his more human speeches are normally preceded by _Shy_. The character is assigned eighty speeches in Q1, including one (4.1.398-400) that is clearly not his. Roughly two-thirds (54) of these speeches are preceded by _Shy_ (or _Shyl_, _Shylocke_); the remainder (26) are preceded by _Iew_ (or _Iewe_). In the stage directions he is "_Shylocke_ the Iew" when he first enters (1.3), _Iewe_ (_Iew_) in 2.5 and 3.3 (twice), and _Shylocke_ in 3.1 and 4.1. One might suspect that since the type for Q1 was set up by two compositors, their separate preferences would have been responsible.[32] However, both used the personal rather than the generic name most of the time, Compositor X 15 times to 10 and Compositor Y 39 times to 16. Y set up the courtroom scene from line 143 to the end (H1-H4^V), using _Iew_ for one speech, _Shy_ for the next seven, _Iew_ for nine of the next ten, and _Shy_ for eight of the last nine.

The pattern of prefixes is as follows. In 1.3 Shylock is _Shy_ (_Shylocke_) for six speeches as he discusses the bond with Bassanio, but _Iew_ for the next three as he asks to speak with Antonio, indignantly rejects the idea of eating with Christians, and delivers his aside on Antonio, beginning "How like a fawning publican he looks!"; thereafter he is _Shy_ (_Shyl_) for the rest of the scene. In 2.5 he is _Iewe_ in his first speech as he tells Launcelot--in traditional usurer fashion--that the latter will not "gurmandize" with him any more, but then _Shy_ for the rest of the scene with Launcelot and his daughter. (However, the first speech is in Compositor X's stint, the rest by Compositor Y; they might be responsible for the transition in this instance.) In 3.1 he is _Shy_ (_Shyl_, _Shylocke_) throughout as he is tormented by Salerio and

Solanio, pleads for his right to revenge, and converses with Tubal. As the cruel usurer who will not listen to Antonio in 3.3 he is _Iew_ in both stage directions and prefixes. Finally, in the courtroom scene, he is _Shylocke_ in the direction but _Iewe_ (_Iew_) in his first ten speeches, which are harsh and aggressive. The last _Iew_ is before line 176, where he says, "Shylock is my name," and thereafter he is _Shy_ for seven unrelenting speeches, as if the use of his name reminded the writer of the individual person. But as Portia apparently acknowledges the validity of the bond, he becomes the cruel, triumphant _Iew_ (250) who in nine of the next ten speeches provides the scales of justice but not the surgeon of mercy since "Tis not in the bond." In line 314, his first speech after Portia has prevented him from taking more or less than a pound and from shedding blood, his name reverts to _Shy_, then _Iew_ in 318, and finally _Shy_ in 336 for the rest of the play. Once he is defeated he is again the individual rather than the generic _Iew_.

The most likely explanation is that these speech prefixes are authorial and, if so, that they reflect either Shakespeare's own attitude toward the character at a particular point in the play or the attitude he expected to create in his audience by the speeches he was writing (or both). As the wicked, hard-hearted hater of Antonio called for by the flesh-bond plot, Shylock is the generic Jew, both religious and economic. However, on other occasions--when he discusses Jacob, describes how he is spat upon by Antonio, speaks to his daughter, is ridiculed by Salerio and Solanio, protests that Jews are human, and has become the loser in the courtroom--the dramatist presents him as an individual named Shylock.

If the playwright favored <u>Shylock</u> over <u>Jew</u> by about two to one, the characters in the play prefer <u>Jew</u> over <u>Shylock</u> by more than four to one (61 to 15). In 1.3, when the Christians want to borrow money from him, they call him by his personal name four times and use <u>Jew</u> twice with careful irony ("And say there is much kindness in the Jew" and "Hie thee, gentle Jew"). In the first part of the courtroom scene, as they are trying to dissuade him from pursuing his revenge, the Christians call him by his proper name five times and <u>Jew</u> thirteen times; once he is defeated he is always <u>Jew</u> (eleven instances), though the prefixes call him <u>Shy</u>. In Acts 2, 3, and 5 the characters call him by his generic name 35 times, his individual name only six times. (No doubt we should recognize that in verse scenes the characters' terms may sometimes be influenced by the playwright's preference for a one-syllable or a two-syllable word in his pentameter line.)

Shylock's personal name probably has connotations of ethnic and religious Jew and of usurer. Although much effort has been expended in the search for its source and meaning, no widely accepted solution has been found. One possibility frequently mentioned is Israel Gollancz's proposal, endorsed by George L. Kittredge, that <u>Shylock</u> is derived from <u>shallach</u>, which is Hebrew for cormorant;[33] the usurer is referred to as a cormorant in Munday's <u>Zelauto</u> and elsewhere in Elizabethan literature. On the other hand, William M. Merchant suggests that the name is "a semi-morality term, Shy-Lock, implying secrecy and hoarding."[34] However, such a superficial meaning seems unworthy of the character Shakespeare created. An Old Testament name would seem the obvious choice.

There is a better suggestion of where Shylock came
from that has not received the recognition it deserves,
probably because it has been attached to an unlikely
theory. In 1871 Karl Elze suggested that the name came
from the Hebrew Shelach in Chapters 10 and 11 of
Genesis; he pointed out that three other Jewish names
in the play (Tubal, Chus, and Jessica) probably also
come from the same chapters.[35] Believing that English
Bibles translated the name Salah (as does the King
James version, for example), he thought Shakespeare
must have consulted a Hebrew source. Cardozo took up
the point in 1925, observing that Shakespeare did not
read Hebrew and postulating an Hebraist or Greek
scholar, who, he supposed, had used the name first in
the non-extant play The Jew mentioned by Gosson.[36]
However, this elaborate explanation is not necessary:
in Genesis 10.24 the Geneva Bible declares that
"Arpachshad [the son of Shem, the grandson of Noah]
begate Shelah, and Shelah begate Eber," and it adds in
the margin, referring to Eber, "Of whome came the
Ebrewes or Iewes."[37] Shelah is mentioned four more
times in Genesis 11.12-15.

The name Shelah seems eminently suitable for
Shakespeare's Jew, since Shelah was the father of the
eponymous founder of the "Ebrewes" and an ancestor of
Jacob. In adapting the name, Shakespeare could
exercise his fondness for puns and humour names,
playing on the humour or "semi-morality" combination
Shy and Lock, suggesting apartness, secrecy, and
hoarding--all characteristics appropriate for his
usurer. Perhaps, too, he was aware of a pun on
shallach. If, as Cardozo suggests, the y of Shylock is
pronounced as short i, the name sounds more like Shelah
and shallach, though the pun on Shy disappears. As an

adaptation of <u>Shelah</u> with rich implications of Jew and usurer, the name <u>Shylock</u> is not unworthy of the character it describes.

Two further associations or "sources" for Shylock remain to be considered briefly, Pantaloon and Marlowe's Barabas. Although Kathleen M. Lea cautioned against assuming that the influence of Pantaloon (<u>Pantalone</u>)--a standard character in the <u>Commedia dell'arte</u>--on Shylock was direct, John R. Moore found that "all the accessible illustrations of Pantaloon resembled the accepted figure of Shylock" and suggested that Pantaloon is one "brightly colored thread" out of which Shylock is woven.[38] Pantaloon is often a widower and is robbed by his daughter or son, who elopes with a disapproved lover. He considers his male servant a huge eater, and sometimes the servant's father intercedes for him. He is "always a merchant of Venice," is avaricious, worries about his ships, carries a huge knife, has a large nose, and is often opposed by a doctor named <u>Graziano</u>. Moore observes that (unlike Marlowe's Barabas) Shylock is not considered dangerous before or after he makes his claim: "perhaps the sympathy of the spectators for the father who has lost his daughter and his fortune would have been less poignant for an audience to whom the memory was still fresh of the absurd Pantaloon grieving loudly for the daughter and the ducats he had lost."[39] In his <u>Italian Comedy in the Renaissance</u> Marvin T. Herrick describes Shylock's troubles as especially like those of <u>Pantalone</u> in Scala's <u>La pazzia d'Isabella</u> and <u>Il fido amico</u>.[40] However, since the stage-usurer himself had inherited many of Pantaloon's characteristics, a blend of the two may have been what the playwright had in mind. Shylock seems more vigorous than Shakespeare's "lean and slipper'd pantaloon" in <u>As You Like It</u> a few years later:

> With spectacles on nose, and pouch on side,
> His youthful hose, well sav'd, a world too wide
> For his shrunk shank, and his big manly voice,
> Turning again toward childish treble, pipes
> And whistles in his sound.   (2.7.158-63)

Shylock's debt to Marlowe's Barabas is elusive. Certainly <u>The Jew of Malta</u> cannot have been absent from the playwright's mind. Yet the spirit of Marlowe does not appear in <u>The Merchant</u> (except in the boasting of Morocco), and his Jew is so unlike Shylock that superficial similarities turn out to be differences. Thus, Shylock and Barabas are Jews, but Barabas describes the other Jewish merchants as "silly men" (1.1.177) and despises them along with Christians and Turks, whereas Shylock speaks of his "sacred nation" (1.3.48).   Both are hard, cruel men, but Barabas gloatingly induces people to kill each other, poisons an entire nunnery to eliminate his unfaithful daughter, and blithely sells Christians to Turks and Turks to Christians, whereas Shylock merely wishes to destroy a single man who is a business competitor and who has treated him badly. Both love wealth, but Barabas, who romanticizes it, is an enormously rich merchant who operates on a grand scale, Shylock a mere city money-lender. Barabas is the title character who speaks almost half the lines in a play that is the "Famous Tragedy" of his life, but Shylock has only the second largest role as an unsuccessful antagonist who is ignored for the first three hundred and the last three hundred lines of a comedy named for the man he hates. At the same time, as A. C. Swinburne said, Shylock is "a living subject for terror and pity," Barabas "a mere mouthpiece for the utterance of poetry as magnificent as any but the best of Shakespeare's."[41]

In discussing another matter, Irving Ribner points out that the Jew of Malta is the "defiant heathen wronged" who seeks revenge in a manner corresponding to the way he has been treated and then is himself undone with the same kind of treachery.[42] So the Jew of Venice emphasizes deliberately that he will revenge as Christians revenge, and, hanging his vengeance on a legal technicality, is himself undone by another legal technicality. Possibly The Jew of Malta contributed to the "Hath not a Jew eyes?" passage.

Marlowe's greatest contribution to The Merchant was preparing the way for both Shakespeare and his public. He provided an idea and a challenge for the first. Barabas was a fascinating, distinctive character, whose actions and motivations were unusual and yet more amenable to the willing suspension of disbelief because they came from a type of person who was known to exist yet was hardly ever encountered in England, and of whom fantastic stories were told emotionally involved with the audience's religion. Shakespeare's original audience probably came to the theater expecting something similar. The playwright gave them a character not dissimilar enough to be disappointing but yet so individual that his creator seems to owe hardly any artistic debt to his predecessor.

Shylock has something of each of the "sources" discussed in this chapter. The real "Jews" of London (persons of Hebrew descent who had recently appeared to become Christians) may have contributed to the idea of developing Shylock as a human being and to the

successful realization of that idea; they probably
supplied details of behavior, some of which may also
have come from Shakespeare's reading or hearing about
contemporary Jews abroad.   On occasion, however,
Shylock is the theological Jew who hates Christians and
is thought to be the servant of the devil.   He also has
many characteristics of the usurer, a familiar type in
London life and in the London theater.   Yet he is
called "Jew" rather than "usurer" on the stage, often
with the secondary meaning (and occasionally with the
primary meaning) of extreme hard-heartedness: the word
Jew blends hard-hearted usurer with the religious and
ethnic person.   The directions and prefixes of the play
suggest that, apart from what the characters appear to
think, the playwright had similar attitudes but not
always on the same occasions, reflecting perhaps the
way he wished Shylock to impress his audience at the
moment.   Shylock's failure to fit completely into any
category helps protect him from caricature and
melodrama.

Chapter VII
Shylock in the Play

Although Shakespeare may have chosen to dramatize the pound-of-flesh story partly because it gave him the opportunity to develop the dynamic character of the Jew on the stage, yet, once he had made the choice, he was largely governed by the needs of his chosen plot in the development of the character. The plot is demanding, and one might suspect that the playwright was intrigued by the challenge of its requirements. Moreover, if this thesis is correct, it seems likely that he was less interested than has often been supposed in conveying a message or creating a type, such as a "Jew dog," a representative of a severely persecuted minority, a commentary on usury, a comic villain, a tragic villain, or a pathetic figure. He was above all interested in creating a successful play. In addition, inconsistencies that are sometimes perceived in the presentation of Shylock lose their significance as inconsistencies in the light of the overall design, so that what some commentators have regarded as evidence for Shakespeare's partially rewriting the play ceases to be evidence of that supposition.

As Richard G. Moulton pointed out a century ago, a major problem inherent in the bond plot in a comparatively realistic play is the improbability of the fantastic bond itself, including the difficult motivation of borrower and lender to arrive at and agree upon the conditions.[1] It seems incredible that an experienced, successful merchant should borrow from a hated, despised, vengeful enemy on such potentially lethal terms. It also seems incredible that a professional usurer should not charge his enemy the highest interest rate he could and instead propose-- even think of proposing--a penalty which, though potentially deadly to his enemy, is overwhelmingly likely to remain uncollected (since some of Antonio's ships will surely return in time), and which would then leave the usurer with no interest or profit of any kind on the loan, and the hated borrower with a moral and financial triumph. As we have seen, previous tellers of the story have sometimes ignored the problem. However, a non-dramatic narrator can, without being obligated to supply details, escape with saying that certain matters happened, whereas the dramatist who must stage the scene effectively and present the characters realistically must provide believable persons and conversation. Even granted that the usurer and the merchant could agree on such a fantastic bond, it is hard to believe that the Jewish usurer would actually try to collect from the Christian borrower in a Christian court and that the court would take him seriously.

There are three elements involved in making the bond believable: a believable borrower, a believable lender, and a believable situation and conversation leading one to propose and the other to accept.

Shakespeare's borrower Antonio is believable in that,
first, he is motivated by a friendship such as that in
The Sonnets where the attachment is worth more than
life itself; second, he is melancholy, passive, and
indifferent toward everything but this friendship;
third, he has supreme confidence that at least some of
his many ships will return; and fourth, he cannot
believe that the despised object of his spittle could
possibly be a genuine threat to his life.

There are two obvious ways to make Shylock
acceptable as proposer of the bond: first, he can be
the devil Jew, the theological Jew, and the "Jewish"
(hard-hearted) usurer; anything could be believed of
such a monster, but such a melodramatic character is
himself hardly to be believed. The second is to
develop motives and some degree of sympathy for his
point of view as a human being; this human portrayal
may make him believable, but it hinders sympathy with
the characters to whom he is opposed; it tends to make
the antagonist the dominant figure in the play; and it
still may not be sufficient to account for an
inherently improbable act. Fortunately, the methods
are complementary: the human portrayal of the character
drawn by the second method controls the unbelievability
of the character drawn by the first, and the evil
associated with the character drawn by the first method
controls antagonism toward his opponents while also
supporting the believability of the act. In other
words, the "sources" of Shylock described in the last
chapter must be evoked, yet he should also be motivated
as fully and forcefully as possible in a human way so
that we can in some measure feel his passion for
revenge--a remarkable challenge in presenting a Jew to
a sixteenth-century audience.

As for the believable situation, the conversation between the borrower and the lender should be arranged in such a way that it leads fairly reasonably to the proposal as a "merry sport" that it would be embarrassing for Antonio not to accept. Then in later scenes Shylock's motives for destroying Antonio should be kept before us (Jessica's flight with her father's valuables to marry a Christian acquaintance of Antonio's is an excellent means), and we must continue to feel as well as to understand his emotions. If all this is real enough, our poetic faith may be sufficiently strong to accept the suit in court. However, we should be kept aware simultaneously that Shylock is the antagonist of the friends and lovers in a romantic comedy where he cannot finally succeed; here his being a Jew and a usurer help, and we should be reminded of those facts--but not too much.

There is no preparation for Shylock's appearance; he is on stage dominating the conversation from the first line of scene 3. Although his costume and appearance may reveal that he is a Jew, the character is introduced in his first four speeches as the more familiar usurer going over the terms of a loan coolly and carefully with Bassanio. When Shylock declares Antonio to be a "good man," Bassanio objects indignantly to any question of his friends's (moral) goodness, but the money-lender explains that in his world "good man" means "good risk," and then, like a financial analyst, he proceeds to explain risk: "ships are but boards, sailors but men," and of course there are thieves, pirates, waters, winds, and rocks; still, Antonio is "sufficient." When he asks to speak with the merchant, Bassanio's invitation to dinner replaces the familiar, cautious, passionless usurer with the

angry Jew, who sneers at eating pork and who will buy,
sell, talk, and walk with Christians, but will not eat,
drink, or pray with them. The emphatic tone in which
Bassanio's well-meant if naive invitation is rejected
prepares for the deep antagonism toward Antonio to be
revealed immediately in Shylock's next speech. At this
point the speech prefixes in Q1 shift from Shy to Iew
for three speeches (29-31, 33-39, 41-52).

Antonio's entrance elicits an extended "aside"
from Shylock in which he announces to the audience four
reasons for hating the merchant as well as his general
intention to destroy Antonio if he can. The device
resembles the soliloquies of Richard III (written
earlier), Iago, and Edmund (written later), in which
the aggressor reveals his destructive attitude. As
yet, though, Shylock, unlike Richard, Iago, or Edmund,
has no plan. As Iew in Q1, he says,

> I hate him for he is a Christian;
> But more, for that in low simplicity
> He lends out money gratis, and brings down
> The rate of usance here with us in Venice.
> If I can catch him once upon the hip,
> I will feed fat the ancient grudge I bear him.
> He hates our sacred nation, and he rails
> Even there where merchants most do congregate
> On me, my bargains, and my well-won thrift,
> Which he calls interest. Cursed be my tribe
> If I forgive him.

It is his only significant aside/soliloquy in the play;
he has little need to conceal his purpose beyond this
scene.

The first two reasons for hating Antonio are the
motives of the theological Jew and the greedy usurer.

The first--that Antonio is a Christian--is not directly mentioned again by Shylock, though his sharpening his knife and approaching Antonio to cut the pound of flesh in the courtroom scene must have reminded the playwright's contemporaries of it. Perhaps the single, flat statement was enough for an Elizabethan audience; on the other hand, it appears likely that Shakespeare did not want to emphasize this motive, for it is certainly no way to persuade a Christian audience to see matters from the Jew's point of view. The second motive--Shylock's resentment that Antonio undermines the usurer's business by not charging interest--is from the realistic economic world, in which one hates the successful, "unfair" competition. It is easy to understand why Shylock feels as he does, but the motive arouses no sympathy in an audience some of whom pay but perhaps none of whom (in an Elizabethan audience) receive interest. This second motive is introduced with the words "But more," as if it is the stronger motivation (unless the words mean only "in addition"). Shylock mentions this motive four times in later scenes (3.1.48-50, 55, 127-29, and 3.3.2), and Antonio refers to it in 3.3.21-24.

Although the two statements are bald, they are evidently felt strongly by Shylock, who asserts with an image from wrestling suggesting physical struggle and triumph and an image from eating suggesting satisfaction of strong desire that he will take revenge if he can. The words "ancient grudge" refer back to both motives but suggest especially the Jew's rather than the usurer's hatred. These first two reasons are not responses to anything Antonio has done to Shylock deliberately: they are feelings originating with the Jew-usurer. Since Shakespeare puts them first and has

Shylock indicate that they are sufficient, it seems
that to understand him as merely reacting to the bad
treatment he has received is to oversimplify the
character.

The third and fourth motives are reasons for
"revenge," for they respond to Antonio's deliberate
behavior. That Antonio hates Jews is doubtless true--
it is supported in the scene that follows--but since
Shylock hates Antonio for being a Christian, it seems
like a rationalization. From the modern sociological
point of view it may appear that Christians hated and
Jews responded, but from the theological point of view,
the Jews killed Christ before they were hated. It
prepares for the fourth motive, which has dominated
interpretations of Shylock since the beginning of the
nineteenth century. This last motive combines the
economic with the personal, for Shylock is railed
upon--and spat upon, we discover shortly--in his place
of business, and the "thrift" of which he is proud is
insultingly called "interest." It is this fourth
motive that both individualizes Shylock and will be
expanded over the next seventy lines to persuade us to
see his point of view and to lead toward the making of
the bond. Shakespeare's strategy has been to present
Shylock as usurer and Jew in dialogue and then in
motive before giving him a lively personal reason for
hatred that is readily understandable, that will take
the conversation where it ought to go, and that will
help make the character individual and real. The
speech concludes with an oath, "Cursed be my tribe" if
Antonio should be forgiven, a vigorous addition to the
wrestling and gluttony images.

Shylock is uncertain how to use Antonio's need to
his advantage, and he plays the conventional usurer

when he says he must borrow from Tubal, preparing no
doubt to claim later that Tubal insists on charging
outrageous interest which, with a show of regret, he
must pass on. He has absentmindedly forgotten the
terms ("I had forgot--three months--[to Bassanio] you
told me so"), and then he returns to the bond for eight
words before veering away to tell the story of Jacob
and Laban, which ostensibly has to do with the taking
of interest. His resentment is more powerful than and
distracts him from his concern about the loan itself,
which he will go ahead with only when he has figured
out how to get Antonio "upon the hip" and "feed fat
[his] ancient grudge." As he is venting his feelings
and taking advantage of the fact that the would-be
borrowers have to listen to him courteously for a
change, he is looking for the way.

Since the considerable literature generated by the
controversy over the taking of interest did not employ
the Jacob-Laban story[2] (and even Shylock acknowledges
that Jacob did "not take interest, not as you would say
/ Directly int'rest"), commentators have been puzzled
by the playwright's use of the story in this context.
Genesis 30.31-33 tells how the wealthy Laban, who
generally took advantage of Jacob, agreed to let him
have all the lambs that were born ringstaked, speckled,
or spotted. Normally, there would be few, but when
Jacob planted certain rods before the stronger ewes
while they were conceiving, all their lambs were born
"parti-color'd." The next chapter of Genesis explains
that Jacob received hints that he should act in this
way from a dream of divine origin.

. . . Mark what Jacob did:
When Laban and himself were compremis'd
That all the eanlings which were streak'd and pied

> Should fall as Jacob's hire, the ewes being rank
> In end of autumn turned to the rams,
> And when the work of generation was
> Between these woolly breeders in the act,
> The skillful shepherd pill'd me certain wands,
> And in the doing of the deed of kind,
> He stuck them up before the fulsome ewes,
> Who then conceiving did in eaning time
> Fall parti-color'd lambs, and those were Jacob's.
> This was a way to thrive, and he was blest;
> And thrift is blessing, if men steal it not.

By omitting reference to the dream, Shylock implies that the trick was Jacob's idea; he tells merely "what Jacob did." In the last two lines "Blessing" is "the bestowal of divine favour and prospering influence" (OED, vbl. sb. 3), and "thrift" is "the fact or condition of thriving or prospering" (OED, sb.[1] 1). Thus, for Shylock, Jacob's act was a way to prosper, and he received divine favor, and prospering is divine favor--as long as it is not achieved by stealing.

Antonio's reply provides a different interpretation, expressing the "general opinion of the [Christian] commentaries" that "the 'hand of Heaven' is clearly responsible for the outcome, . . . and Jacob is merely following divine guidance in taking a way of recovering his own property of which Laban had defrauded him":[3]

> This was a venture, sir, that Jacob serv'd for
> A thing not in his power to bring to pass,
> But sway'd and fashion'd by the hand of heaven.
> Was this inserted to make interest good?
> Or is your gold and silver ewes and rams?

Antonio makes Aristotle's distinction between unnatural
and natural breeding, but Shylock promptly answers, "I
cannot tell [whether gold and silver are ewes and
rams], I make it breed as fast"--that is, they are
similar for his purpose. To which Antonio responds
that even "The devil can cite Scripture for his
purpose."

The Jacob-Laban story is relevant in two ways.
First, it is an example for Shylock and for us of
seizing an opportunity against a wealthy oppressor and
(with God's "blessing") achieving success. And second,
it juxtaposes the taking of interest and the taking of
flesh with God's approval. Since the Elizabethan
controversy over interest deliberately stressed the
difference between reproduction of money and of flesh,
Shakespeare's audience would have been accustomed to
hearing them discussed together.[4] If the chance comes
for him to trick his wealthy oppressor, he, like his
Biblical ancestor, will seize it; perhaps God will
enable him to prosper, too.

Having started a train of thought with the example
of Jacob, Shylock ignores Antonio's moralizing and
returns to the subject of the bond: "Three thousand
ducats--'tis a good round sum." But when Antonio
follows his lead ("Well, Shylock, shall we be beholding
to you?"), Shylock changes the subject again:

Signior Antonio, many a time and oft
In the Rialto you have rated me
About my moneys and my usances.
Still have I borne it with a patient shrug
(For suff'rance is the badge of all our tribe).
You call me misbeliever, cut-throat dog,
And spet upon my Jewish gaberdine,
And all for use of that which is mine own.

> Well then, it now appears you need my help.
> Go to then, you come to me, and you say,
> "Shylock, we would have moneys," you say so--
> You, that did void your rheum upon my beard,
> And foot me as you spurn a stranger cur
> Over your threshold; moneys is your suit.
> What should I say to you? Should I not say,
> "Hath a dog money? Is it possible
> A cur can lend three thousand ducats?" Or
> Shall I bend low and in a bondman's key,
> With bated breath and whisp'ring humbleness,
> Say this:
> "Fair sir, you spet on me on Wednesday last,
> You spurn'd me such a day, another time
> You call'd me dog; and for these courtesies
> I'll lend you thus much moneys"?

Again Shylock takes advantage of a rare opportunity to be heard. Without saying so, he justifies revenge on Antonio (as he will do explicitly in his revenge speech in 3.1.53-73), bolstering his resolve as he looks for means. At the same time, this powerful account of his maltreatment provides the detailed development of his fourth reason for hating Antonio that involves the audience in his point of view. In a modern audience it creates considerable sympathy for Shylock. How much it did so for an Elizabethan audience, which was closer in time to the theological attitude toward the Jew, is hard for us to estimate. But Shakespeare, who would have been able to judge his audience's response, must have expected it to have some effect. Perhaps the theological attitude was sufficiently abstract that it interfered less with a specific, well-pleaded case than we might suppose.

Antonio refuses to beg. He retorts angrily that he will continue to spit and spurn, for it is only enemies who lend money at interest, and he expects Shylock to confirm the enmity. "For when did friendship take / A breed for [offspring of, i.e., interest] barren metal of his friend?" asks the merchant. This reply opens the door for Shylock, who sees and swiftly takes his advantage. Ostensibly to be friends, to avoid the spitting and spurning, he will offer the loan without interest (it seems he does not need to borrow the money from Tubal, after all) and, in "merry sport," the forfeit if the loan should not be paid in the right place at the right time will be

> . . . an equal [exact] pound
> Of your fair flesh, to be cut off and taken
> In what part of your body pleaseth me.

When Bassanio expresses doubts, Shylock reassures the Christians with imagery that recalls the ewes and lambs of the Jacob story:

> A pound of man's flesh taken from a man
> Is not so estimable, profitable neither,
> As flesh of muttons, beefs, or goats,

followed by the lie that "To buy his favor, I extend this friendship." The business man Antonio can believe him: it is obviously good business not to be spat upon by the chief Christian merchant in the Rialto "there where merchants most do congregate."

Apologists for Shylock have sometimes taken him at his word, believing that the Jew would like to be Antonio's friend (or at least not an enemy) and that he does not at this point have any intention of taking the pound of flesh.[5] Shylock cannot anticipate that Antonio's ships will not return during the stipulated three months, and we can readily suppose that the Jew's anger hardens after Jessica has eloped with the Christian Lorenzo. But such apologists have been sympathizing with Shylock rather than reading the play. There seems little point in Shylock's earlier aside, his desire to "feed fat" his grudge, his curse on his tribe if he should forgive, unless we are to understand that he pursues his revenge relentlessly, however he may dissemble. Later, Jessica will testify that he planned to take the pound of flesh even before she fled from his house. As for the improbability that all Antonio's ships will be lost or delayed, it is a small chance but the best that he has. Probably, as Norman Nathan has suggested, Shylock hopes that God will bless him as He blessed Jacob[6]--and indeed for a time it seems that God is doing so!

Perhaps it is more realistic to think that in addition to embarrassing Antonio, morally obligating him to treat Shylock better, and giving him something to worry about, Shylock gloats over the small chance that the merchant might default. If he should, Shylock would have power over his enemy in ways not yet fully worked out in his mind, such as further embarrassing Antonio, forcing him out of the practice of lending money free of interest, threatening to collect the penalty and accepting a large bribe from the Christians instead (Bassanio offers such a bribe in the courtroom scene), or (delicious fantasy) actually cutting the flesh from his enemy. There are many half-open doors down the corridor, and the possibilities will give Shylock pleasant thoughts until Antonio's ships return.

Thus, the strategy of the scene has been to present Shylock briefly as conventional usurer and theological Jew but then to develop him at greater length as an individual with his own point of view, his attitude toward what he euphemistically calls "usance," his admiration of and his identification with Jacob, and his powerfully expressed feeling of indecent treatment at the hands of Antonio. Meanwhile, the conversation develops from a Biblical story initially intended to justify "thrift" but, as it involves the underdog's turning the tables on the wealthy persecutor, suggesting to Shylock that he seize any chance to get revenge himself. When Antonio unintentionally encourages the Jew to forego interest and pose as a "friend," he enables Shylock to suggest with a show of good nature the pound of flesh as a joke. This strategy moves the fantastic story far along the road to realism.

In Act 2, as the bond matures, as Antonio's ships do not return, and as Bassanio makes his way to Belmont, Shylock appears once (scene 5) and is discussed by Launcelot, Jessica, Salerio, and Solanio (scenes 2, 3, and 8). If Launcelot describes Shylock as a "devil," Jessica thinks his house is "hell" and Launcelot "a merry devil" in it (2.3.2). When her father tells her to close his doors and windows so that she cannot look out and the sound of drum and fife cannot enter his "sober house" (2.5.29-36), one has the impression that Jessica is allowed little joy in her life. Like Old Capulet, Shylock has no idea that he is playing the heavy father in his daughter's love match, but even much less than Capulet would he approve if he did know. Shylock appears at a disadvantage in other ways in 2.5. He will go to dinner with the Christians in order to help spend their wealth, though he had refused on principle earlier. He is comically superstitious: "There is some ill a-brewing towards my rest

/ For I did dream of money-bags to-night" (2.5.17-18).
And he is suspicious, mistrustful, and proverbially
thrifty:

> . . . Well, Jessica, go in,
> Perhaps I will return again immediately.
> Do as I bid you, shut doors after you;
> Fast bind, fast find--
> A proverb never stale in thrifty mind.
>   (2.5.51-55)

At this point in the play he is Shy-Lock.

In 2.8 Solanio describes Shylock's rage on finding
that Jessica and Lorenzo have escaped him. The
account, which is both a comic description and an
obviously hostile, probably exaggerated picture,
controls our emotional response, so that we are amused,
sympathetic, and disgusted at the same time:

> I never heard a passion so confus'd,
> So strange, outrageous, and so variable
> As the dog Jew did utter in the streets.
> "My daughter! O my ducats! O my daughter!
> Fled with a Christian! O my Christian ducats!
> Justice! the law! my ducats, and my daughter!
> A sealed bag, two sealed bags of ducats,
> Of double ducats, stol'n from me by my daughter!
> And jewels, two stones, two rich and precious
>   stones,
> Stol'n by my daughter! Justice! find the girl,
> She hath the stones upon her, and the ducats."
>   (2.8.12-22)

For Shakespeare and his audience, the scene must have
raised the spirit of Marlowe's comic Barabas, who
cries,

> O my girl,
>
> My gold, my fortune, my felicity,
>
> . . .
>
> O girl! O gold! O beauty! O my bliss!
>
> [He] hugs his bags.   (2.1.47-54)

By having Solanio report the speech (instead of having Shylock speak it), Shakespeare mutes the comic melodrama of Shylock's paraphrasing Barabas in a reverse context (Barabas is receiving the gold from his daughter as he speaks his lines).

The picture of Shylock in Act 2 as harsh employer and angry father-usurer serves several purposes. By giving him a household, Shakespeare renders him more human and so less melodramatic and more familiar and, therefore, ultimately more threatening in his revenge. Jessica's flight with a Christian husband and his "Christian ducats" adds in a dramatic way to his motivation. At the same time the unpleasant characteristics he reveals, the frequently comic context, and the traditionally unsympathetic roles he plays in the act keep him at a distance.

After a scene of one hundred lines in Belmont, Solanio and Salerio appear again in 3.1; as they lament Antonio's losses, they are interrupted by "the devil . . . in the likeness of a Jew" (19-21). In taunting him about the loss of his daughter and then challenging his intentions with regard to Antonio, they emphasize the relationship between the two matters. Indeed, Shylock describes Antonio as "another bad match" (44), the first bad match being his relationship with his daughter.[7] Stung by Salerio's assumption that he will not really take Antonio's flesh ("What's that good for?"), Shylock replies,

To bait fish withal--if it will feed nothing
else, it will feed my revenge. He hath
disgrac'd me, and hind'red me half a million,
laugh'd at my losses, mock'd at my gains,
scorn'd my nation, thwarted my bargains,
cool'd my friends, heated mine enemies; and
what's his reason? I am a Jew. Hath not a
Jew eyes? Hath not a Jew hands, organs,
dimensions, senses, affections, passions; fed
with the same food, hurt with the same
weapons, subject to the same diseases, heal'd
by the same means, warm'd and cool'd by the
same winter and summer, as a Christian is?
If you prick us, do we not bleed? If you
tickle us, do we not laugh? If you poison
us, do we not die? And if you wrong us,
shall we not revenge? If we are like you in
the rest, we will resemble you in that. If a
Jew wrong a Christian, what is his humility?
Revenge. If a Christian wrong a Jew, what
should his sufferance be by Christian
example? Why, revenge. The villainy you
teach me, I will execute, and it shall go
hard but I will better the instruction.

(3.1.53-73)

Critics have seen this speech from different
points of view. Romantically, for Harley Granville-
Barker it "is the theme for a greater play than
Shakespeare was yet to write";[8] for Charlton it is "a
revelation of [Shylock's] profound humanity, his sense
of community of Jew and Gentile, though now that sense
expresses itself distortedly as a partly demented
sufferer's opportunity to wreak bitter revenge on those
who have narrowed the bonds of human sympathy by

excluding from it the race to which he belongs."[9] More severely, Palmer warns that "what is commonly received as Shylock's plea for tolerance is in reality his justification of an inhuman purpose."[10] Michael Echeruo cautions that "European persecution of the Jews was not based on the belief that Jews were not capable of feeling pain. The pathos of Shylock's statement would in all certainty, then, be absorbed as a genuine but irrelevant protest, an evasion of the major issues in dispute," which Echeruo defines as "his self-confessed hatred of Christ (and Christians) and his unbridled usury."[11]

The opening lines of the speech reiterate the last three motives for hating Antonio listed by Shylock in his aside in 1.3.: economic competition ("He hath . . . hind'red me half a million"), Christians' hatred of Jews ("scorn'd my nation"), and the persecution he has received. The rest of the speech is a plea for human treatment which, if not granted, will inevitably result in inhuman retaliation. It is based on the Old Law-- "an eye for an eye" of the Old Testament. It is "justice" without mercy. As a contradiction of the New Law of forgiveness in the New Testament, it anticipates Portia's speech on mercy and Shylock's negative response in Act 4. It is also a rationalization of judicial murder: Shylock will not kill in order to imitate Christians (who have not tried to kill him), but to achieve satisfaction for less than capital wrongs. He would "better the instruction," become more sinning that sinned against. In terms of the plot, the speech's function should be clear. Now that Shylock is about to implement the fantastic terms of the bond, we must be made to feel his motivation again in the most powerful way possible. The speech sounds human, and the more human he seems and the more articulately he presents his case before the action moves to the courtroom, the more willingly the audience will suspend its skepticism in Act 4.

In the remainder of 3.1 Shakespeare presents Shylock at a disadvantage, as if to counteract any sympathy raised by his long speech:

> Why, there, there, there, there! A diamond
> gone, cost me two thousand ducats in
> Frankford! The curse never fell upon our
> nation till now, I never felt it till now.
> Two thousand ducats in that, and other
> precious, precious jewels. I would my
> daughter were dead at my foot, and the jewels
> in her ear! Would she were hears'd at my
> foot, and the ducats in her coffin!
>
> (3.1.83-90)

Even allowing for exaggeration under stress, his concern for his riches over his daughter is absurd and ironic in one who has just pleaded so forcefully for humanity. He gloats over Antonio's losses (97-107), agonizes over his daughter's extravagance with his wealth (110-12), rejoices over Antonio's difficulties again (116-17), and pathetically laments the loss of a ring his wife Leah had given him as a young man (120-23), only to forget that loss in more gloating over Antonio, arranging the arrest of the merchant for the economic reason rather than for revenge after all ("for were he out of Venice I can make what merchandise I will," 128-29), and appointing a rendezvous with Tubal in the synagogue. Despite the human, individual touch of his wife's turquoise, it is an unpleasant picture of the man's values and passions. Since Shylock's behavior rarely prompts a neutral response and often provokes conflicting reactions, he is a lively, interesting, individual, controversial character, well able to fulfill his functions in the play.

We both hear and see more of Shylock before the courtroom scene. When Salerio and Jessica arrive in Belmont, the former describes the Jew's recent behavior in Venice:

> . . . Never did I know
> A creature that did bear the shape of man
> So keen and greedy to confound man.
> He plies the Duke at morning and at night,
> And doth impeach the freedom of the state,
> If they deny him justice. Twenty merchants,
> The Duke himself, and the magnificoes
> Of greatest port, have all persuaded with him,
> But none can drive him from the envious plea
> Of forfeiture, of justice, and his bond.
>
> (3.2.274-83)

Jessica follows immediately with her testimony that her father is serious about taking Antonio's flesh. Both speeches prepare us directly for Shylock's adamant behavior in the courtroom.

The next scene (3) is a dress rehearsal. Shylock (or _Iew_ as the stage directions and speech prefixes of Q1 call him) refuses to listen to pleas for mercy. He has taken an oath to have his bond (line 5), thereby making his pursuit of it even more certain, and he plays up to the hard-heartedness described by Salerio:

> I'll not be made a soft and dull-ey'd fool
> To shake the head, relent, and sigh, and yield
> To Christian intercessors. Follow not,

I'll have no speaking, I will have my bond.
(3.3.14-17)

Antonio contributes two points: that Shylock's motive
is mainly economic ("I oft deliver'd from his
forfeitures / Many that have at times made moan to me,"
22-23) and the Duke's need to follow the law to
maintain Venice's reputation with strangers. As Alfred
Harbage points out, Shylock has now humiliated Antonio;
from here on he moves "to mete out a kind of punishment
in excess of the kind of injuries received."[12]

The courtroom scene (4.1) opens with the Duke of
Venice's description of the hard-hearted Jew (Iew in
the first ten speech prefixes) as we last saw him in
3.3:

        A stony adversary, an inhuman wretch,
        Uncapable of pity, void and empty
        From any dram of mercy.   (4.1.4-6)

Called into the court, Shylock is told that "the world"
expects him to show mercy at the last moment instead of
his "strange apparent cruelty" and even to "Forgive a
moi'ty [portion] of the principal." From what we have
seen of Shylock's frame of mind, this expectation is so
absurd that we anticipate his harsh rejection of it.
Despite its absurdity the appeal must be made because
the strategy of the scene is not only to save Antonio,
but also to give Shylock every possible chance to
change his mind, or, if he persists, to let him go so
far that he can no longer withdraw.

The Jew's reply is not designed to elicit
sympathy. He has already told the Duke what he intends
and has sworn by the Sabbath to do it; he dares the
Venetians to risk their "charter" by denying him.[13] He
imagines that they ask why he persists and then

impudently refuses to explain beyond saying that it is his "humor" (whim or ruling characteristic). He then gives four unpleasant examples of "humors" that may seem extravagant to others: paying ten thousand ducats to get rid of a rat, avoiding a "gaping pig" (either as served at the table or as hung up by a butcher after its throat has been cut), avoiding being driven mad by beholding a cat, and becoming incontinent upon hearing a bagpipe. So, says Shylock, he has given no reason-- and **will** not--beyond hating and loathing for Antonio in pursuing what is admittedly a "losing suit." It is a provoking speech, designed to antagonize both characters and audience, well prepared for by what we have seen previously of Shylock's hatred. From the playwright's point of view, if Shylock and his case have not been made credible by this point in the play, it is too late. He is now entirely the antagonist, as the speech prefixes suggest.

Antonio replies that arguing with "the Jew" is like trying to control the tide or persuading the wolf not to steal the lamb or forbidding the mountain pines to be silent when the wind blows through them--images of the inevitability of nature which are like the hardness of Shylock's "Jewish heart" (80). He submits. Bassanio is quick to offer Shylock six thousand ducats--twice the amount of the loan--thereby reminding the Jew, the court, and us that the usurer not only faces no loss of principal but also has the chance of a large profit. Stressing the point, Shakespeare has Shylock reject even six times Bassanio's offer, which would be twelve times the loan or an 1100% profit in three months. "How shalt thou hope for mercy, rend'ring none?" asks the Duke, and Shylock replies, "What judgment shall I dread, doing no wrong?" By "wrong" Shylock means violating the law in its narrowest, literal sense, excluding ideas of equity or fairness; earlier he had taken the similarly narrow view that the only restriction on blessed thrift is not stealing. The Duke's question and Shylock's reply place Old and New Testament viewpoints in epigrammatic opposition; they prepare for Portia's more extended treatment of the subject later in the scene.

In further answer to the Duke, the Jew compares his ownership of a pound of Antonio's flesh to the Venetians' harsh treatment of slaves:

> . . . You will answer
> "The slaves are ours." So do I answer you:
> The pound of flesh which I demand of him
> Is dearly bought as mine, and I will have it.
>   (4.1.97-100)

The Duke, faced with this justification of a wrong by a wrong, his own lack of arguments, and the Jew's demand for "judgment" (103), threatens to postpone the trial until he has further legal advice. Fortunately, it arrives in the next sixty lines as the disguised Portia is introduced. So far the Jew has triumphed, and his success has made the bond and threat more real even as he has been losing whatever sympathy there may have been for him earlier. As Portia presents her credentials, Shylock sharpens his knife (121-22). This is a dramatic action, traditionally exploited by actors on the stage. Charles Macklin, who played Shylock with great success from 1741 to 1789 seemed so malignant at this point that, according to theater lore, his audience shuddered, King George II had difficulty sleeping, and on one occasion, a young man in the pit fainted.[14]

When Antonio acknowledges the bond, Portia asserts, "Then must the Jew be merciful." (The secondary meaning of _Jew_ as hard-hearted person sharpens the paradox.) The sentence is open to at least three interpretations: the Jew must be compelled to be merciful; the Jew is obliged (from the Christian point of view, as all other human beings on earth) to be merciful; or we must persuade the Jew to be merciful. Shylock, recognizing only the law, naturally takes it in the first sense: "On what compulsion must I? tell me that" (183). Portia's reply takes it in the second or third (or both): "The quality [characteristic quality] of mercy is not strain'd [forced, constrained],"

It droppeth as the gentle rain from heaven
Upon the place beneath. It is twice blest:
It blesseth him that gives and him that takes.
'Tis mightiest in the mightiest, it becomes
The throned monarch better than his crown.
His sceptre shows the force of temporal power,
The attribute to awe and majesty,
Wherein doth sit the dread and fear of kings;
But mercy is above this sceptred sway,
It is enthroned in the heart of kings,
It is an attribute to God himself;
And earthly power doth then show likest God's
When mercy seasons justice. Therefore, Jew,
Though justice be thy plea, consider this,
That in the course of justice, none of us
Should see salvation. We do pray for mercy,
And that same prayer doth teach us all to render
The deeds of mercy. I have spoke thus much
To mitigate the justice of thy plea,
Which if thou follow, this strict court of Venice

> Much needs give sentence 'gainst the merchant
> there.

(4.1.184-205)

The speech is an impressive statement of central
Christian ideas about mercy: it blesses both giver and
receiver; it is more becoming in the more powerful; in
exercising it mankind imitates God; and all of us
exercise mercy because we hope for it ourselves. But,
she repeats in her conclusion, mercy cannot be forced;
Portia can only plead with the Jew, and if he will not
yield, the court must decide against Antonio. As
expected, Shylock sweeps away the chance: "My deeds
upon my head! I crave the law, / The penalty and
forfeit of my bond."

It has been objected that such an emphatically
Christian appeal is misdirected at the Jew. But except
for Shylock all the people in the Venetian courtroom
and the Elizabethan theater are Christians, all paying
at least lip-service to these ideas, and both
Shakespeare and Portia are obliged to keep the main
principles before them--to keep decorum. Since the
tables are about to be turned on the nearly victorious
Shylock, it is dramatically suitable to remind
everybody that they ought to be turned on him--in
principle, not just by technicalities. As Portia has
said, the Jew "must" be merciful. Moreover, as noted
previously, Shylock is to be given every chance to
change his mind, and Portia promptly confirms that he
has been offered a good profit to forgo his revenge.
Bassanio offers thrice and even ten times the sum and
pleads that "To do a great right" the Duke or Portia
"do a little wrong" by overriding the law. Clear-
sighted about the dangers of such a course, Portia
refuses. Again money is offered and again rejected,

this time with Shylock's insistence that he has "an oath in heaven" not to relent. Shylock is asked whether he has scales ready to weigh the flesh, and he is indeed prepared with those symbols of justice. He is asked to provide a physician "for charity," but he refuses since it is not in the bond. Antonio reminds everyone that he is dying for the high principle of friendship; Bassanio extravagantly declares that he would sacrifice himself and his wife for the same principle; and Portia moves on to the sentence.

"Tarry a little," says Portia, "there is something else," and in this speech and two others to follow she not only prevents Shylock from collecting the pound of flesh, but she also turns the tables on him:

> This bond doth give thee here no jot of blood;
> The words expressly are "a pound of flesh."
> Take then thy bond, take thou thy pound of flesh,
> But in the cutting it, if thou dost shed
> One drop of Christian blood, thy lands and goods
> Are by the laws of Venice confiscate
> Unto the state of Venice.   (4.1.306-12)
> . . .
>
> Therefore prepare thee to cut off the flesh.
> Shed thou no blood, nor cut thou less nor more
> But just a pound of flesh. If thou tak'st more
> Or less than a just pound, be it but so much
> As makes it light or heavy in the substance
> Or the division of the twentith part
> Of one poor scruple, nay, if the scale do turn
> But in the estimation of a hair,
> Thou diest, and all thy goods are confiscate.
> . . .   (324-32)

> Tarry, Jew,
> The law hath yet another hold on you.
> It is enacted in the laws of Venice,
> If it be proved against an alien,
> That by direct or indirect attempts
> He seek the life of any citizen,
> The party 'gainst the which he doth contrive
> Shall seize one half his goods; the other half
> Comes to the privy coffer of the state,
> And the offender's life lies in the mercy
> Of the Duke only, 'gainst all other voice.
>
> (346-56)

The first two speeches grant Shylock his pound of flesh but introduce conditions that discourage him from collecting it. The conditions are from the original story--the sources of the bond plot--and result in using a trick of the law to defeat a man who has tried to use the law for his own destructive purpose. Both Shylock and Portia could be seen as interpreting the law with excessive rigidity, Shylock to destroy a life, Portia to save it. However, by giving the Jew the right to collect the bond (even if at a prohibitive cost), Portia not only avoids violating or neglecting the law, but she reaffirms it in that the lender is still entitled to his bond. As several scholars have pointed out, the process is broadly analogous to the situation in England where, since the fourteenth century, a litigant could receive in the common law courts a judgment against his opponent, who could then appeal to the Chancellor in the Court of Chancery for relief from what he claimed was a harsh, harmful, or incorrect decision. If the Chancellor decided in favor of the appellant, he would not overturn the decision at common law but would inform the litigant that he would

be imprisoned if he attempted to enforce his common law
judgment.[15]   In The Merchant a similar process occurs:
after Portia refuses Bassanio's plea that she waive the
law, she grants the bond as if at common law and then
imposes conditions that have the effect of preventing
Shylock from enforcing his harsh judgment.   Probably
Shakespeare and his audience were conditioned to think
of the process as a way of maintaining the law even as
it was modified with equity or mercy.   The point is not
that   Portia   is   really   following   English   legal
procedure,   but   merely   that   her . verdict   can   be
understood   better   in   the   context   of   the   common   law
courts and the Court of Chancery in Shakespeare's day.
And in much the same sense that the common law is not
overthrown, Shylock is not constrained to show mercy
but does so of his own will.   He still could take the
flesh.

     Only after Shylock has accepted his defeat and is
preparing to leave does Portia invoke the law to punish
him for his attempt on the life of a Venetian.   If she
had shown him the full measure of his loss in the first
of the three speeches, he might have decided to keep
his   vow   and   kill   Antonio   no   matter   what   the
consequences.   From that point of view the sequence is
psychologically appropriate.   Of course, the Duke or
Portia might have used the law earlier, but then the
scene would have been truncated, and Shylock would not
have had the full opportunity to change his mind.   With
the law against attempted murder Shakespeare caps the
traditional means of defeating the usurer with a hint
of the real world, in which the court would not have
listened seriously to the Jew's plea and, if he had
made very clear his intention to kill, might have
accused   him   of   attempted   murder.   With   a   pseudo-

realistic law the playwright reverses the situation on Shylock so completely that it is now his life that is in jeopardy.

The greater realism of character and bond call for serious punishment of Shylock. In comedy the defeated antagonist is normally punished in suitable ways, as in his pocket-book if he is an usurer, and is compelled to acknowledge the values of the victors. In pre-Shakespearean versions of the bond story the money-lender loses what he lent, but as long as he does not attempt to collect the bond, he is not punished otherwise. Only in Cursor Mundi is the Jew threatened with loss of his goods and his tongue; his revealing the true cross saves him from both penalties as he becomes a Christian. The lenders in Dolopathos and Zelauto voluntarily reward the borrower with a gift of money or the opportunity to inherit. None of these possibilities is enough for Shylock, who has seriously tried to kill Antonio; the more successful Shakespeare's efforts to achieve realism, the more surely must the Jew endure the consequences. Moreover, punishing Shylock recovers the impression of a human being that had been overlaid by the hard-hearted Jew since the first scene of Act 3. Moulton calls Shakespeare's technique here "dramatic hedging" and observes, "So successful has Shakespeare been in the present instance that a respectable minority of readers rise from the play partisans of Shylock."[16]

The speech prefixes in Q1 change from Iew to Shy in line 314 ("Is that the law?" after he is told that he must not shed blood) except for 318, but the characters call him "Jew," never "Shylock," for the rest of the play. The punishment tests the Christians: given the opportunity to apply harsh justice, they

"must" show mercy. From their point of view, they do.
Portia lists three penalties: Shylock's life is at the
Duke's mercy; one half his fortune comes to the state;
and the other half his fortune comes to the man he had
attempted to kill, Antonio. The Duke gives Shylock his
life before he can ask for it, pointing out that this
is more than Shylock would do for the merchant, and the
half his fortune owed the state is reduced to a fine.
Thinking his ships are lost, Antonio takes the other
half with the intention of turning it over (perhaps the
principal only) to Jessica's husband upon Shylock's
death. Antonio attaches two conditions, which the Duke
endorses. The first is that Shylock make a will,
leaving everything to his only daughter and her
husband. He is not to be allowed to punish his
daughter or prevent her natural inheritance because she
married a Christian for love. Truculento in _Zelauto_
also makes his son-in-law his heir.

Antonio's second condition is that Shylock become
a Christian. He is forcibly given a chance to save his
soul, to belong to the religion of mercy, and to give
up his hard-heartedness--a firm way of compelling the
antagonist in a comedy to accept the values of the
victors and become Antonio's "friend." This condition,
which is so shocking to modern readers, was probably
much less so to the original audience of the play.
Since all Jews who came to England were legally
required to become Christians, it would have seemed not
unreasonable: if Shylock had been living in London, he
would have been a Christian already. Jews in _Cursor_
Mundi and _Le Miracle de un marchant et un juif_ also
become Christians, though voluntarily, at the end of
the story. Audiences and readers are reminded of what
the Christians could have done by Gratiano's preference

for a jury of twelve "godfathers" to bring Shylock "to the gallows, not to the font" (4.1.400).

In the previous analysis I have attempted to show that the playwright develops the character of the Jew pragmatically to render as realistic as possible the proposal of the flesh bond and the Jew's perseverance in attempting to collect it, while at the same time he does not ignore the character's role as antagonist in the play. These practical aims result in his presenting Shylock with conventional associations of theological Jew, hard-hearted Jew, and stage usurer on some occasions--all at least partially lost on a modern audience that is not prepared for them. On other occasions Shylock is presented with some sympathy for his point of view, especially his resentment of unfair treatment. For later generations increasingly sensitive to the treatment of persecuted groups, this aspect of the character has grown in importance as the conventional associations with unreal types have lost their force. But for Shakespeare's day, too, Shylock was built from apparently conflicting points of view which are often reflected in the speech prefixes and stage directions of Q1. The aim was to make him real, at least partly for the purpose of making the flesh bond real. If we do not limit ourselves to one side of the picture by seeing him as persecuted victim or as melodramatic villain, he fills his role remarkably well as the least unlikely man behind the unlikely flesh bond.

Chapter VIII
Shylock: The Critics and the Playwright

The discussion in the last chapter largely ignores two questions that many readers will consider more important than the one it attempts to answer. First, even if Shakespeare's handling of Shylock was mainly pragmatic, how is the character to be interpreted in the reader's mind and on the stage? And second, why is the portrayal of Shylock as vivid, dynamic, and successful as it is, and does not its striking success indicate that Shakespeare's heart was in it well beyond the needs of his plot?

If we may think of the dramatist as intending that Shylock be regarded not primarily as theological Jew or hard-hearted usurer ("Jew") or comic or malignant villain or pathetic figure, but as including and emphasizing each of these as it is needed, the character is more lifelike, for people under pressure in dramatic emotional situations (such as a sensational trial) may project comic, malignant, or pathetic images of themselves at different times and to different observers, none of them fully true or untrue. I have suggested that Shakespeare created such a character because of the needs of his plot, but the result, whatever the cause or degree of intention, is to produce an unusually complex and lifelike character. If so, the whole wealth of response to Shylock on the stage and in the study is relevant to our understanding of him, in somewhat the same way that a collection of impressions of a major leader from many persons who knew that leader under differing circumstances may approach the real, complex person much more nearly than any one impression. What follows is a brief critical history of Shylock as viewed through the interpretations of actors and the eyes, minds, and imaginations of theater and literary critics.

In 1600 the title page of the first edition of The Merchant (Q1) advertised the book's contents as follows:

> The most excellent Historie [presumably
> meaning "story"] of the Merchant of Venice.
> With the extreame crueltie of Shylocke the
> Iewe towards the sayd Merchant, in cutting a
> iust pound of his flesh: and the obtayning of
> Portia by the choyse of three chests.

Neither the play nor the Jew is described as comic, though the head title on the first page of text and the running title throughout the book is "The comicall History of the Merchant of Venice." In the First Folio the play is entitled merely "The Merchant of Venice," but it is included in the section headed "Comedies." We do not know for whom the role of Shylock was written. T. W. Baldwin considers it "a characteristic part for [Thomas] Pope," who was "the high comedian and gruff villain of the company."[1] The presumed Collier forgery, On the Death of the Famous Actor, Richard Burbadge, assigns the role to Burbage--Collier's

assumption, it would seem.[2] Lelyveld suggests Burbage
or Kempe.[3] Since Kempe was known for his clown roles
and probably played Launcelot as successor to Launce,
and since the conventional wisdom is that Burbage
played romantic leads in comedies (here, Bassanio),
Pope seems a more likely choice. The associations with
usurer and Pantaloon suggest a comic emphasis; yet
presumably Shakespeare's fellow-actors generally
conveyed their chief playwright's intentions, which--if
we have understood them rightly--keep Shylock from
remaining in any conventional slot for long.

Shakespeare's romantic comedies were not popular
during the Restoration, and there is no record of even
an adaptation of The Merchant on the stage until 1701,
when George Granville's The Jew of Venice: A Comedy was
first performed and published.[4] This adaptation was
played frequently until 1741, when Shakespeare's
Merchant returned to the stage, replacing it. A number
of scholars have preferred to doubt that Granville's
Shylock was primarily comic, but there can be little
doubt: the role was originated by Thomas Doggett, a
comic actor, and John Downes, actor, prompter, and
theater historian, wrote in 1708 that Doggett was "the
only Comick Original now Extant: Witness . . . The Jew
of Venice."[5] A year later Nicholas Rowe complained
that "tho' we have seen [The Merchant, by which he
means Granville's adaptation] Receiv'd and Acted as a
Comedy, and the Part of the Jew perform'd by an
excellent Comedian, yet I cannot but think it was
design'd Tragically by the Author."[6] In this respect
Rowe was a generation ahead of his time.

Granville's Shylock is less individual and human
as well as more hypocritical and vindictive than
Shakespeare's. He merely refers briefly to the story

of Jacob without telling it; he is exaggeratedly
friendly as he proposes the bond; he does not talk with
Launcelot (who is omitted from the adaptation) or with
Tubal (also omitted); he is not described by Salerio
and Solanio (they, too, are omitted); and he addresses
the revenge speech to Antonio after the latter is
arrested. In the courtroom scene he says gloatingly
that he knows Bassanio will have to hang himself if
Shylock succeeds in killing Antonio. He is not
compelled to become a Christian. By far the longest
scene in Granville's version is a new one in which
Shylock goes to dinner with the Christians. He gives
two speeches, in the first of which he drinks to his
"Mistress" money after Antonio has toasted his friend,
Bassanio has toasted Portia, and Gratiano has toasted
women. In the second speech he grotesquely observes
aside that the embraces of Antonio and Bassanio as they
part remind him of his affection for his money.
J. H. Wilson rightly describes Granville's character as
"a petty villain of an exaggeratedly melodramatic
type," an overreaching, stock-jobbing Jew, who was
"intended to evoke laughter."[7]

Between Granville's adaptation and E. E. Stoll's
major twentieth-century statement of the comic view of
Shylock, almost all British critics and actors thought
Shylock either a serious villain or a tragic figure.
However, a few German critics believed the character
was intended to be comic: Hermann Ulrici found "rather
a decidedly comic impression," especially in the
passage with Tubal and in the courtroom scene, where
"his whole being, his appearance, his manner of
expressing himself in word and gesture, are obviously
described intentionally in such a way as always to
verge upon caricature."[8] Georg Brandes felt that "to

the Elizabethan public, with his rapacity and his
miserliness, his usury and his eagerness to dig for
another the pit into which he himself falls, [Shylock]
seemed, not terrible, but ludicrous." Brandes thought
Shakespeare was more sympathetic but could not express
his true feelings because his public would have been
"bewildered and alienated," and the censor might have
intervened.[9]

Stoll's substantial essay was first published in
1911.[10] The author thought that not only did
Elizabethans see Shylock as comic, but that Shakespeare
intended him that way: "By all the devices . . . of
Shakespeare's dramaturgy Shylock is proclaimed . . . to
be the villain, though a comic villain or butt." "He
is . . . a trickster, a whining and fawning hypocrite,
and he sweareth to another man's hurt and changeth to
avoid his own." He is forgotten in Act 5; he is given
the harsh treatment accorded the villain, harsher than
in other versions of the bond story; everyone except
Tubal speaks ill of him; and his intention of taking
the pound of flesh is horrifying. The motives he
expresses in his aside; his use of specious arguments,
such as the Laban story and his reply to the Duke in
4.1.35-62; his being "a miser, a money-lender, a Jew";
his wishing his daughter dead and shifting his grief
from daughter to ducats; his being referred to as the
"devil"--all make the case against him. Stoll cites
earlier drama, the Lopez affair, the demands of the
story, and Elizabethan attitudes toward Jews and usury.
Of the "Hath not a Jew eyes?" speech, Stoll says that
to be pathetic it should be addressed to someone
sympathetic and that Shakespeare's villains normally
plead their cases: "He is only defending himself in
what he intends to do; we make him defend his race

against all that has been done to it. He is putting in a plea for the right of revenge; we turn it into a plea for equal treatment at the outset." Stoll notes such comic devices as Gratiano's jeering, "the anti-climaxes and prompt miserly afterthoughts of Shylock, comical on the face of them, and the whetting of his knife." Stoll's view is uncompromising: "in the Shylock scenes there is so large an element of formal external comic technique that it is impossible to consider Shylock only 'semi-humorous,' in part pathetic."[11]

As a corrective to the almost exclusively sympathetic criticism of his day, Stoll's interpretation was important, but he was insensitive to the complexity of both the playwright's technique and the resulting creation. He has had followers, some more absolute than others. Hazelton Spencer, citing Stoll, agreed that Shylock was "the comic butt" and suggested that he was played with a large nose and shrugs and grimaces. He thought the role was much like that of the villain in Victorian melodrama, "who plots, gloats, curses, and ha-ha's his way through to the final scene, when he is exposed, foiled, disgraced, and ridiculed, till he expires, leaves town, or at best slinks off stage with a futile imprecation."[12] The playwright's efforts to make the Jew real seem to have failed utterly with Spencer.

Others--such as John Palmer, C. L. Barber, and Edgar Rosenberg--accept the premise of the comic Jew but qualify it. For Palmer, "The imaginative effort expended by Shakespeare in making his Jew a comprehensibly human figure has imparted to him a vitality that every now and then stifles laughter and freezes the smile on our lips. If these passages are rightly handled by the actor or accorded their just

place and value by the reader, the comedy remains
intact. If . . . [they] are thrown into high relief
and made to stand out of their context, the comedy is
destroyed."[13] For Barber, Shylock's "role is like that
of the scapegoat . . . in whom the evils potential in a
social organization are embodied, recognized and
enjoyed during a period of licence, and then in due
course abused, ridiculed, and expelled." For the
Elizabethans "to understand did not necessarily mean to
forgive. Shylock can be a thorough villain and yet be
allowed to express what sort of treatment has made him
what he is."[14] For Rosenberg, Shylock "moves in an
atmosphere of laughter--but of apprehensive laughter:
tentative, wary, inhibited." He is not pure miser or
butcher: "the type is just flexible enough to permit of
mutations, changes in posture, adjustments in perspec-
tive, and to generate, here and there, a small shock of
surprise."[15] These critics' unwillingness to take
absolute positions brings them much closer to the
complexity of the character.

The view that Shylock's villainy far outweighs--if
it does not completely obscure--any compensating
qualities, and that he is to be regarded as a serious
rather than a comic character has been expressed
frequently in both the eighteenth and the twentieth
centuries. We have seen Rowe's opinion in 1709 that
Shylock should not be played comically. He added that
there is "such a deadly Spirit of Revenge [in the
play], such a savage Fierceness and Fellness, and such
a bloody designation of Cruelty and Mischief, as cannot
agree either with the Stile or Characters of Comedy."[16]
In the following year the dramatist and critic Charles
Gildon observed briefly that "The Character of the Jew
is very well distinguish'd by Avarice, Malice,

implacable Revenge, &c."[17] In 1741 Charles Macklin
realized this conception of the character on the stage
in Shakespeare's Merchant (displacing Granville's
adaptation); he was to play the role for forty-eight
years.   John Doran described Macklin's hugely
successful first night: "As the play proceeded, so did
his triumph grow.   In the scene with Tubal, which
Doggett in [Granville's] version had made so comic, he
shook the hearts, and not the sides of the audience.
There was deep emotion in that critical pit."[18]
Alexander Pope reportedly told Macklin enthusiastically
that he played Shylock as "the Jew that Shakespeare
drew."[19]   Macklin was admired, too, by Francis
Gentleman, who wrote in 1770, "Shylock . . . is a most
disgraceful picture of human nature; he is drawn, what
we think man never was, all shade, not a gleam of
light; subtle, selfish, fawning, irascible and
tyrannic." Normally a sensible critic, Gentleman found
that in the courtroom scene "the retorts of Gratiano
are admirably pleasant, and the wretched state to which
Shylock is in his turn reduced, is so agreeable a
sacrifice to justice, that it conveys inexpressible
satisfaction to every feeling mind; the lenity of
Antonio is judiciously opposed to the malevolence of
his inexorable persecutor."[20]

Extreme as Gentleman's view may appear, Muriel
Bradbrook, writing 181 years later, is hardly less
vigorous. For the Elizabethans, Shylock's motives were
no more justification for his actions than Richard
III's crooked birth or Edmund's illegitimacy are for
theirs: "Nothing less monstrous than the theatre's
prize bogyman [i.e., the Jew], linked in the popular
mind with Machiavelli and the Devil in an infernal
triumvirate, would serve for the villain of a romantic

comedy. Were he less diabolic, Shylock would not be tolerable." "In Shylock [Shakespeare] has drawn a man lapsing into beast."[21]

A larger number of modern scholars see Shylock as serious economic villain. For Leo Kirschbaum, "The force of events was creating Economic Man--but not, as yet, his justification. . . . Shakespeare set before his definitely Anglican, definitely patriotic, and definitely conservative audience a monster, Shylock, in whom disruptive individualism, economic aggrandizement, and perturbing uncanniness appear at their most frightening and melodramatic." Of Shylock's ill-treatment Kirschbaum says, "To Shakespeare and his audience sociological determinism was never a valid cause. It was always a villain's excuse."[22]

Two other scholars with similar views were cited in Chapter VI in connection with the background they provide for Shylock. Warren D. Smith believes that "What Shakespeare is really trying to do through Shylock is to depict a character who rationalizes his villainy, as a usurer, by projecting his own ethnic group prejudice onto the shoulders of his innocent opponents." He points out that the Christians do not maltreat the Jew on stage, that Antonio maltreats him elsewhere because he charges interest, and that the term Jew may refer to his being an usurer. Shylock is not a "truly religious Jew" because he eats with Christians, plots vengeance in a synagogue, does not keep his oath to kill Antonio, and rates the Jews' sufferings below his ducats (3.1.83-86). "To the dramatist, surely, he was above all a hypocrite who concealed his innate evil behind the mask of a religion he himself did not believe in." Although Smith's points about Shylock's maltreatment may be true and he

may project his prejudice, his opponents are certainty
not without prejudice themselves. The flaws in his
Jewishness seem overstressed. Shakespeare is doing
much more than "really trying . . . to depict a
character who rationalizes his villainy, as a
usurer."[23]

Grebanier thinks that Shylock's usury is more
important than his Jewishness. However, since he lacks
some of the characteristics usually assigned to the
stage usurer, he is not caricatured. "Shylock was
perforce a villain, but he must be also a villain
entitled to respect to a degree, a man with his own
dignity and perspectives. A lesser figure could have
done no justice to the grand idea which was
Shakespeare's preoccupation in the play." Grebanier
overreacts to Stoll's interpretation, asserting in
italics that "Shylock is not amusing at any moment of
the play." In the scene with Tubal "it is Tubal who is
comic" as he alternately depresses and raises Shylock's
spirits.[24] Although Grebanier recognizes some of the
character's complexity, his is a partial, limited view
of Shylock.

In the anonymous collection, Essays by a Society
of Gentlemen, at Exeter (London, [1796]), a writer
identifying himself as "T. O." undertook what is
apparently the first substantial defence of Shylock.
He saw Shylock as cruel because of the ill-treatment he
has received and his daughter's flight. The Mosaic
Law--his law--entitled him to an eye for any eye, and
the laws of Venice permit him no occupation but usury.
"Shylock's feelings are certainly neither laudable, nor
consonant to the purity of our religion; yet they are
not unnatural to any one in his situation. He does not
appear, knowingly, to violate any divine or human law,

but boldly avows, in conscious integrity, before a Court of Judicature, that 'he dreads no judgment doing no wrong.'"[25] But the interpretation originating with Macklin was still dominant, and the reviewers were no more tolerant of T. O.'s defence of Shylock than they were to be of Wordsworth and Coleridge's Lyrical Ballads two years later. One reviewer replied that Shylock is what "all readers and spectators" have taken him to be, and another observed that "as an usurer [Shylock] cannot consistently be an object of abhorrence in a land of stock-jobbers: but, as an insidious contriver of murder, we hope that he will never be regarded with a mitigated detestation."[26] In reply to T. O.'s enthusiastic defence of Shylock, one might point out that "Thou shalt not kill" is a divine and human law that Shylock must have known.

The appearance of Edmund Kean as Shylock in 1814 was a significant step. Two passages from William Hazlitt--the first his reaction to Kean's interpretation, the second his own understanding of the character--emphasize the change from the Macklin tradition and set out the interpretation of a major Romantic critic:

> When we first went to see Mr. Kean in
> Shylock, we expected to see, what we had been
> used to see, a decrepid old man, bent with
> age and ugly with mental deformity, grinning
> with deadly malice, with the venom of his
> heart congealed in the expression of his
> countenance, sullen, morose, gloomy,
> inflexible, brooding over one idea, that of
> his hatred, and fixed on one unalterable
> purpose, that of his revenge. We were
> disappointed, because we had taken our idea

from other actors, not from the play. . . .
That [Shylock] has one idea, is not true; he
has more ideas than any other person in the
piece; and if he is intense and inveterate in
the pursuit of his purpose, he shews the
utmost elasticity, vigour, and presence of
mind, in the means of attaining it. But so
rooted was our habitual impression of the
part from seeing it caricatured in the
representation, that it was only from a
careful perusal of the play itself that we
saw our error.[27]

In proportion as Shylock has ceased to be a
popular bugbear, 'baited with the rabble's
curse,' he becomes a half-favourite with the
philosophical part of the audience, who are
disposed to think that Jewish revenge is at
least as good Christian injuries. Shylock is
a good hater; 'a man no less sinned against
than sinning.' If he carries his revenge too
far, yet he has strong grounds for [it],
which he explains with equal force of
eloquence and reason. He seems the
depositary of the vengeance of his race; and
though the long habit of brooding over daily
insults and injuries has crusted over his
temper with inveterate misanthropy, and
hardened him against the contempt of mankind,
this adds but little to the triumphant
pretensions of his enemies. There is a
strong, quick, and deep sense of justice
mixed up with the gall and bitterness of his
resentment. . . . The desire of revenge is

almost inseparable from the sense of wrong;
and we can hardly help sympathising with the
proud spirit, hid beneath his 'Jewish
gaberdine,' stung to madness by repeated
undeserved provocations, and labouring to
throw off the load of obloquy and oppression
heaped upon him and all his tribe by one
desperate act of 'lawful' revenge, till the
ferociousness of the means by which he is to
execute his purpose, and the pertinacity with
which he adheres to it, turn us against him;
but even at last, when [he is] disappointed
[and harshly treated], we pity him, and think
him hardly dealt with by his judges.[28]

The idea of Shylock as tragic figure reached its
climax in the theater with Henry Irving in 1879, whose
interpretation is somewhat undercut by the comment of
the theater critic William Winter, who reported that
Irving said in Winter's presence, "'Shylock . . . is a
bloody-minded monster,--but you mustn't play him so, if
you wish to succeed; you must get some sympathy with
him.'"[29]   Winter described Irving's changing
interpretation:

When Irving first acted Shylock he manifested
a poetically humanitarian ideal of the part,
and . . . he indicated the Jew as the
venerable Hebrew patriarch, the lonely,
grieved widower, and the affectionate, while
austere, father. [Shylock was] the vengeful
representative antagonist of intolerant
persecution of the Jewish race and religion,
but [Irving] personated a man, originally
humane, who had become embittered by cruel

injustice, without having entirely lost the
essential attributes of average
humanity. . . .   In the fundamental,
propulsive motive of his performance there
was more of racial oppugnancy than of
personal hatred. As time passed, however, a
radical change in the personation was, little
by little effected, till at last, without
entire abandonment of a purpose and power to
awaken sympathy, it became the true <u>Shylock</u>
of Shakespeare--hard, merciless, inexorable,
terrible. Thus matured, Irving's <u>Jew</u> was a
man upon whom,--while his every thought was
colored and every purpose directed by racial
antipathy and religious fanaticism,--social
oppression had so wrought as to develop only
the most radically evil propensities.

Irving's exit at the end of the courtroom scene was
especially effective:

<u>Shylock</u> moved slowly and with difficulty, as
if he had been stricken by fatal weakness and
were opposing it by inveterate will. At the
door he nearly fell, but at once recovered
himself, and with a long, heavy sigh he
disappeared. The spectacle was intensely
pathetic. . . .[30]

The omission of the fifth act on the stage for much of
the nineteenth century emphasized the overriding
interest in Shylock at the expense of the rest of the
play.

Many twentieth-century critics have interpreted
Shylock sympathetically. For Cumberland Clark,
"Shylock almost appears to glow with a certain superi-

ority beside the wastrel friends of Antonio. . . . He is the only one who seems to have any real fixity of purpose, and his enslavement to the idea of revenge and consequent defeat become a tragedy indeed."[31] To Harold Goddard, though Shylock was "made cruel by the insults" of Antonio and others and "driven to desperation by his daughter, there is nothing to indicate that Shylock was congenitally coldhearted, cruel, or desperate. On the contrary, it is clear that he had it in him, however deep down, to be humane, kindly, and patient, and his offer to Antonio of a loan without interest seems to have been a supreme effort of this submerged Shylock to come to the surface. . . . Shylock was the leaden casket with the spiritual gold within."[32]

Although most commentators before 1900 and some since have taken one of the three views of Shylock described above, there are many in this century who have regarded him as a complex character, perhaps open to different interpretations simultaneously (a viewpoint similar to that of this book), or as being too substantial a figure for the background against which he appears, or as resulting from revision and changing dramatic purpose. Several of these views are discussed briefly below.

In 1929 Ashley Thorndike described Shylock as "a monster like the giants and dragons of story-land" on the stage, "an avenging villain and the proper butt of the Christians" from the point of view of "Elizabethan stage practice," and "a many-sided man, whose revenge is not without justification, whose wrongs weigh against his crimes, and whose contest with his persecutors gains a dignity because he fights single-handed the battle of his race. The result is not

strict consistency of characterization, rather it is
richness of personality. Shylock will not stand
precise analysis by either Elizabethan or modern
psychology, but our continued questioning of his
motives and meanings indicates how vital and
interesting he still is after three centuries."[33]

Five years later H. B. Charlton, in an essay that
has become well-known, asserted that Shakespeare
"planned a **Merchant of Venice** to let the Jew dog have
it, and thereby to gratify his own patriotic pride of
race." Charlton thought that although the playwright
"never doubted that he had made, a Shylock fit only for
exciting execration and opprobrium," this character and
the Shylock "who wrings the withers of a modern
audience are both in the play." The story demanded a
monster, but a dramatized version required a man.
Shylock can be seen as appealing for understanding
through his defence of usury and his account of his
sufferings. He is driven to revenge by the flight of
his daughter with his ducats, and it is not until his
long speech in 3.1 justifying revenge that he considers
actually collecting his bond. Shylock "has been
transformed into the intelligible fanatic who with
perfect naturalness may play the pathetically demented
role he must fulfil in the trial scene. He provides an
admirable example of the way in which the dramatist's
instinct secures dramatic reality."[34] Some of
Charlton's points are well taken; but if the analysis
advanced in Chapters VI and VII above is correct, it is
unlikely that the playwright "planned . . . to let the
Jew dog have it" and that he never doubted that he had
succeeded. For reasons given previously, it is
impossible to believe with Charlton that the playwright

thought Shylock did not consider taking the pound of flesh until Act 3.

John Middleton Murry's essay, which appeared two years after Charlton's, is also well known and frequently anthologized. Murry provides a useful concept and phrase when he says, "the method of Shakespeare's drama consists, essentially, in the humanization of melodrama." He notes that Shylock is made unsympathetic in relation to Jessica but sympathetic for "a truly dramatic contrast" with Antonio. "Shylock is both the embodiment of an irrational hatred, and a credible human being. He is neither of these things to the exclusion of the other. And if we ask how that can be? the only answer is that it is so."[35]

Hardin Craig and Madeleine Doran suggest that the Elizabethan fondness for debate contributed to the complexity of Shylock. Craig observes that "Shakespeare, like other Elizabethans, was used to disputation and was a genius at seeing both sides of every issue, and it is the excellence of Shylock's defense which has perplexed the critics and set the play awry."[36] Doran develops the point: "I would not deny that Shakespeare's great gift of imaginative sympathy was chiefly responsible for all that is favorable in the portrayal of Shylock. At the same time I would suggest that the habit of mind fostered by a disputatious age would make such an unresolved presentation of opposing points of view acceptable, and perhaps less recognizable as harmful to dramatic structure than to us."[37] As we have seen, one of the versions of the bond plot that Shakespeare is likely to have known--Discourse 95 in The Orator--is in the form of a debate.

Critics have expressed in various ways the feeling that Shylock is out of balance with the other characters and the plot. Arthur Quiller-Couch thought Shylock "takes charge of his creator, fenced in by intricacies of plot and finding outlets for his genius where he can."[38] Benedetto Croce rejected both the comic and the pathetic interpretations of Shylock, yet the character "arouses some doubt in our minds" because the romance provides an inadequate background: "The reader is not convinced by the rapid fall of so great an adversary, who accepts the conversion to Christianity finally imposed upon him." Croce attributed the inconsistencies to Shakespeare's concentration on character and lack of "particular ideals."[39] These critics emphasize that the ingredients of Shylock's character produced to satisfy the needs of the plot have coalesced into something that transcends the play.

Harold R. Walley found divergent styles in The Merchant that, he thought, indicated revision of the play. He suggested that in this revision "Shakespeare's purpose, in part, was to replace his first Jewish monster with a dramatically plausible human being," perhaps because of declining anti-Semitism after the Lopez affair. He finds the earlier conception in the jailor scene (3.3) and the courtroom scene. The later Shylock appears in 1.3, where Shylock is "the mortal man possessed of a treacherous mind and a grievance," as well as in Act 2 and in 3.1.[40] However, if the demands of the plot created these different Shylocks, there seems little reason to postulate a revision.

From the point of view of this book, John R. Brown's essay originally published as "The Realization of Shylock: A Theatrical Criticism" and later with

alterations as "Creating a Role: Shylock," is
congenial. Brown develops the thesis that the
principal interpretations in the theater "exploit
opportunities given to the actor by Shakespeare." He
concludes,

> By many devices Shakespeare has ensured that
> in performance Shylock is the dominating
> character of the play; none other has such
> emotional range, such continual development,
> such stature, force, subtlety, vitality,
> variety; above all, none other has his
> intensity, isolation, and apparent depth of
> motivation. The various interpretations that
> have become famous do not overgo the intended
> impressions.[41]

Therefore, the role should be played for all that it is
worth.

Actually, the various interpretations probably do
"overgo the intended impressions" of the playwright.
Each of the stereotypes (stage usurer, etc.) and genre
types (comic villain, etc.) that the dramatist used has
been extended by actors and critics and, especially, by
modern scholars attempting to recover a particular
Elizabethan Shylock by study of one type. In their
intensity and (often) exclusiveness, each extension
goes beyond what the playwright probably expected and
the originator of the role on the stage actually
provided. Yet it is closer to the overall pattern of
Shakespeare's Shylock as he is understood in this book
to think of the character from all these extended
points of view (all types) than to think of him from
any single one. What we have seen of Shakespeare's
"sources" for Shylock, the alternation of Shy and Iew

in the speech prefixes in Q1, the analysis in Chapter VII of the character's speeches and behavior in the context of the plot, and the history of the character in the theater and in criticism, all point toward the conclusion that Shakespeare intended a full use of the possibilities of the role.

The weight of the character has also shifted in ways that Shakespeare could not have foreseen. During the last two centuries there has been increasing sensitivity to the persecution of minorities, as well as increasing sympathy with the underdog and with sociological and psychological causes of behavior that often seem to justify what is unjustifiable in any other terms. With these changes Shylock has been in an extraordinarily advantageous position to take on a symbolic reality that extends beyond what his creator created. At the same time attitudes toward money and money-lending have changed so that even though usurers remain unpopular, Shylock's attitude toward lending seems no worse than realistic, whereas Antonio's seems impossibly idealistic and therefore absurd. Shylock's opponents have become less real in other ways and less sympathetic. Today, for example, self-sacrificing friendship is not a generally admired ideal and is frequently supposed to be homosexuality, and the young man who spends excessively and wants to marry money is perceived to be merely an idle and selfish fortune-hunter. "Virtue" of various kinds is regarded with less esteem and more skepticism, as Portia is accused of cheating about the caskets. With the play sometimes stood on its head as far as the characters are concerned, Shylock seems more real, less unjustified, and considerably more relevant in contrast with his surroundings than he was earlier. Even the reality

Shakespeare gave him has altered his position in the play: realism itself in literature has had a higher value since the rise of the novel in the eighteenth and nineteenth centuries. In short, some of the brilliance of Shylock is due to changes in the eye of the beholder.

This is a partial, though only a partial answer to the other question raised at the beginning of this chapter: why the portrayal of Shylock is so vivid, dynamic, and successful, and whether its quality indicates some special interest of Shakespeare's. There are no absolute answers to the question, and the second part especially depends very much on one's general impression of the playwright in relation to his work.

One consideration is that Shakespeare was driven by the unusual needs of his plot to develop Shylock in a more complex and realistic way than had been demanded of him for any character he had created previously. He had no models, and the example that came closest to being a potential model--Marlowe's Barabas--was not suitable for his purpose. The challenge of doing something fresh, individual, and successful with conventional materials seems again and again to have stimulated his best work. Thus, Hamlet evolved out of the conventions of the revenge play, Falstaff out of the Lollard Oldcastle, King Lear out of the anonymous True Chronicle History of King Leir, the history plays out of the chronicle plays, The Tempest out of the dramatic romance, and the poet's love for a young man and infatuation with a dark lady in The Sonnets out of the ennobling Petrarchan love conventions traditionally inspired by a beautiful, blond woman. In other words, the challenge stirred him deeply, and I have tried to show how he responded in Chapter VII.

He may have delighted in seeing what he could accomplish with the various "sources" of Shylock, without intending to "say" anything about Jews or usurers or about prejudice (which his age generally did not regard as prejudice). That he "felt" what he had Shylock say as he wrote the speeches is suggested both by the effectiveness of the lines and by the shifting speech prefixes, but he was trained to do that as professional actor and playwright: he probably "felt" what he had Richard III, Iago, and Edmund say, too, as he wrote their most effective soliloquies. Insight into the Jew's mind was necessary to make the character and the plot work. But as John Keats and many other readers have emphasized, Shakespeare's works generally show little desire to teach or to convey a specific message on the part of the dramatist, and the evidence of the play itself does not make Shylock an exception.

Notes

[1] On the stage history of Marlowe's _Jew of Malta_, see N. W. Bawcutt, ed., _The Jew of Malta_, Revels ed. (Manchester: Manchester UP, 1978) 1-4. In his _Diary_ Philip Henslowe recorded 36 performances from February of 1592 to June of 1596; 8 were in the first six months of 1596 (_Henslowe's Diary_, ed. R. A. Foakes and R. T. Rickert [Cambridge: Cambridge UP, 1961] 16-47).

[2] Unless otherwise indicated, Shakespeare's works are quoted from _The Riverside Shakespeare_, ed. G. Blakemore Evans _et al_. (Boston: Houghton Mifflin, 1974).

[3] Ed., _The Merchant of Venice_, Arden ed. (London: Methuen, 1955) xxvii.

[4] Oxford University Press has published a facsimile of Q1 (Shakespeare Quarto Facsimiles, No. 2, 1957) with an introductory note by W. W. Greg.

[5] See John R. Brown, "The Compositors of _Hamlet_ Q2 and _The Merchant of Venice_," _Studies in Bibliography_ 7 (1955) 17-40.

[6] For example, W[alter] W. Greg, _The Shakespeare First Folio_ (London: Oxford UP, 1955) 256-58; Brown, Arden ed. xiv; Evans 283.

Chapter II

[1] Geoffrey Bullough, <u>Narrative and Dramatic Sources of Shakespeare</u>, 8 vols. (New York: Columbia UP, 1957-75) I: 446, and Bernard Grebanier, <u>The Truth about Shylock</u> (New York: Random House, 1962) 99-100.

[2] Henry Goudy, "Roman Law," <u>Encyclopaedia Britannica</u>, 11th ed. (New York, 1911) 23: 551-52. See also W. W. Buckland, <u>A Textbook of Roman Law from Augustus to Justinian</u>, 2nd ed. (Cambridge: Cambridge UP, 1932) 618-20.

[3] Gosson, <u>The Schoole of Abuse</u> (London, 1579) sig. C6^v.

[4] Dekker's <u>Jew of Venice</u> was entered in <u>S.R.</u> 9 September 1653. Henslowe 23-28. Frederick G. Fleay, <u>A Chronicle History of the Life and Work of William Shakespeare</u> (London, 1886) 30, 197 suggested that Henslowe was referring to Dekker's play.

[5] Jacob L. Cardozo, <u>The Contemporary Jew in the Elizabethan Drama</u> (Paris, 1925) 271-73, provides the Latin text of the flesh-bond story from <u>Dolopathos</u>. My source is the modern translation by Brady B. Gilleland of <u>Dolopathos</u> (Binghamton, New York: Center for Medieval and Early Renaissance Studies, 1981) 55-58.

[6] John Janzems, "Structure and Meaning in the <u>Seven Sages of Rome</u>," <u>Studies on the Seven Sages of Rome</u>, ed. H. Niedzielski <u>et al</u>. (Honolulu: Educational Research Associates, 1978) 43.

[7] Richard Morris, ed., <u>Cursor Mundi</u>, Part IV, Early English Text Society, Original Series 66 (London, 1877) 1226-35.

[8] J. Madison Davis and Sylvie L. F. Richards, "The Merchant and the Jew: A Fourteenth-Century French Analogue to <u>The Merchant of Venice</u>," <u>Shakespeare Quarterly</u> 36 (1985): 63.

[9] E. K. Chambers, <u>The Mediaeval Stage</u>, 2 vols. (London: Oxford UP, 1903) 2: 52-56; see also Karl Young, <u>The Drama of the Medieval Church</u>, 2 vols.

(Oxford: Oxford UP, 1933) Chapter XXI, "The Procession of the Prophets," 2: 125-71.

[10] The Castle of Perseverance concludes with such a scene. See Robert G. Hunter, Shakespeare and the Comedy of Forgiveness (New York, Columbia UP, 1965) 13-21; Lawrence Danson, The Harmonies of "The Merchant of Venice" (New Haven: Yale UP, 1978) 67-69.

[11] Corpus Christi plays died out in the 1560s and 1570s: see Harold S. Gardiner, S.J., Mysteries' End (New Haven: Yale UP, 1946) Chapter V.

[12] John Weld, ed., Gesta Romanorum (Delmar, NY: Scholars' Facsimiles and Reprints, 1973) v.

[13] Cardozo 275-79.

[14] Weld vi.

[15] S. J. H. Herrtage, ed., The Early English Versions of the "Gesta Romanorum," Early English Text Society, Extra Series 33 (London, 1879) 158-65.

[16] Available in W. C. Hazlitt, A Select Collection of Old English Plays, 4th ed. (London, 1874) 6: 245-370.

[17] W. C. Hazlitt 6: 357.

[18] Bullough 1: 476.

[19] Thomas Warton, Observations on the Faerie Queene of Spenser (London, 1754) 94-97 made the suggestion first. Speculation continues about the relationship between the ballad and Wilson's play and between them and the non-extant Jew mentioned by Gosson. Bullough (1: 450) thinks The Three Ladies may have been an answer to The Jew and that the ballad derives from the latter. Kenneth Muir, The Sources of Shakespeare's Plays. (London: Methuen, 1977) 88 suggests that the ballad may be influenced by The Three Ladies and The Merchant.

^{20} _The Pepys Ballads_, 8 vols. (Cambridge: Harvard UP, 1929-32), 1: 16-17.

^{21} John R. Brown, Arden ed. 154. Brown prints the full text of the ballad.

^{22} Bullough 1: 450.

^{23} Grebanier 136-45.

^{24} With rusty high-school French and Latin and a stale year of college Italian, I found the story easy to translate. Brown and Bullough provide their own translations.

^{25} The story is quoted from my (unpublished) translation based on the 1554 edition.

^{26} Jack Stillinger, ed., _Anthony Munday's "Zelauto The Fountaine of Fame"_ (Carbondale: Southern Illinois UP, 1963) 159.

^{27} Janet Spens, _An Essay on Shakespeare's Relation to Tradition_ (Oxford, 1916) 24, first suggested a play. See also Celeste Turner, _Anthony Mundy_ (Berkeley, 1928) 33 and Stillinger's "Introduction" to his ed. of _Zelauto_, xxi.

^{28} Brown, Arden ed. 157 and Muir, _Sources_ 88.

^{29} Bullough 1: 486. Grebanier 112.

^{30} Francis Douce, _Illustrations of Shakespeare and of Ancient Manners_, 2 vols. (London, 1807) 1: 280. Turner 100-2, [196].

^{31} Muir, _Sources_ 87; Bullough 1: 451, 482. The text of Declamation 95 is in Bullough and also in Brown's Arden ed.

Chapter III

^{1} Pre-Shakespearean versions of the flesh-bond story designed for the stage (if there were any) may have substituted the caskets story. The argument that the joining of the two plots must be Shakespeare's because it is so well done is doubly flawed: other dramatists sometimes did very well, and even if the job was done poorly in an earlier play, Shakespeare may have improved it; he usually did. Nevertheless, the fusion of the plots does seem like what Shakespeare achieves elsewhere without help, and I would bet on its being his. Hereafter I will generally assume it is Shakespeare's.

[2] Bullough 1: 511-14 gives the text of the _Gesta_ story but not the moral with which it concludes from Madden's 1838 edition of the _Gesta_ manuscripts; Brown, Arden ed. 172-74 provides selections from the text and moral from Robinson's printed edition of 1595. The entire 1595 _Gesta_ has been edited in facsimile by John Weld (Chapter II, note 12), from which I quote (pp. 95-104).

[3] Bullough 1: 458.

[4] G. C. Macaulay, ed., _The English Works of John Gower_, Early English Text Society, Extra Series 82 (London, 1901) Liber Quintus: lines 2273-2434. _Confessio Amantis_ had been printed by Caxton (1483) and twice by Berthelette (1532, 1554).

[5] Bullough 1: 10 and 6: 354.

[6] Bullough 1: 456-57, 497.

[7] "Mediaeval Prototypes of Lorenzo and Jessica," _Modern Language Notes_ 44 (1929): 227-29.

[8] Celeste Turner Wright, "Some Conventions Regarding the Usurer in Elizabethan Literature," _Studies in Philology_ 31 (1934): 176-97, and "The Usurer's Sin in Elizabethan Literature," _Studies in Philology_ 35 (1938): 178-94. Also Grebanier 91.

[9] "Launce and Launcelot," _Journal of English and Germanic Philology_ 30 (1931): 506-7.

Chapter IV

[1] Allardyce Nicoll, Masks, Mimes, and Miracles (New York: Cooper Square, 1963) 253, 256-60 and Giacomo Oreglia, The Commedia dell'Arte, tr. L. F. Edwards (New York: Hill and Wang, 1968) 84-86. John Florio, A Worlde of Wordes (1598; Hildesheim: Olms, 1972), s.v. Gratiano.

[2] Ed., The Merchant of Venice, New Shakespeare (Cambridge: Cambridge UP, 1926) 100-4.

[3] "Salerio, Solanio, Salarino and Salario," Names 23 (1975): 56-57.

[4] "'The Three Sallies' Reconsidered: A Case Study in Shakespeare's Use of Proper Names," Shakespeare Studies (Shakespeare Society of Japan) 15 (1976-77): 62.

[5] C. T. Onions, A Shakespeare Glossary (Oxford: Oxford UP, 1911) cites The Tempest 2.1.55, where the ground is described as "tawny," as well as "orange-tawny" yarn from A Midsummer Night's Dream 1.2.94.

[6] "Racial Terms for Africans in Elizabethan Usage," Review of National Literatures, 3.2 (Fall, 1972): 54-60.

[7] Danson 73-76; John S. Colley, "Launcelot, Jacob, and Esau: Old and New Law in The Merchant of Venice," Yearbook of English Studies 10 (1980): 181-89.

[8] Wilson, New Shakespeare 99; Brown, Arden ed. xxii, 3.

[9] Karl Elze, Essays on Shakespeare, tr. L. Dora Schmitz (London, 1874) 281.

[10] "Shakespeare's Shylock," Shakespeare Quarterly 15 (1964): 197.

[11] First pointed out by Elze 282.

12 The numbers are from Marvin Spevack, _A Complete and Systematic Concordance to the Works of Shakespeare_ 6 vols. (Hildesheim: G. Olms, 1968-70) 1: 771, 777, 781.

13 Spevack 757, 762, 789, 803.

14 For example, John H. Long, _Shakespeare's Use of Music: A Study of the Music and Its Performance in the Original Production of Seven Comedies_ (Gainesville: U of Florida P, 1955) 107-8. The matter is debated by Brown, Arden ed. 80; Peter J. Seng, "The Riddle Song in 'Merchant of Venice,'" _Notes and Queries_ 203 (1958): 191-93; by Brown again in _Notes and Queries_ 204 (1959): 235; and by Seng once more in _The Vocal Songs in the Plays of Shakespeare_ (Cambridge: Harvard UP, 1967) 40.

15 _Seven Types of Ambiguity_ (1930; New York: New Directions, 1947) 43-44.

16 _Munera Pulveris_ (1872; New York: Weare and Tyne, 1891) 89-90.

17 Hugh MacLean, "Bassanio's Name and Nature," _Names_ 25 (1977): 57.

18 _Shakespeare the Man_ (New York: Harper and Row, 1973) 113.

19 MacLean 56 suggests _bass_ and _base_; Northrop Frye, _The Anatomy of Criticism_ (Princeton: Princeton UP, 1957) 166 suggests _basanoi_.

20 An excess of black bile was supposed to cause melancholy. Hazelton Spencer, _The Art and Life of William Shakespeare_ (New York: Harcourt Brace, 1940) 244 dismisses speculation bluntly: since "every Elizabethan knew that if you had too much black bile it was your hard luck," further reasons for Antonio's sadness are unnecessary.

Chapter V

1 William Winter, _Shakespeare on the Stage_ (New York: Moffat, Yard, 1911) 186-87 described Irving's dramatic conclusion to 2.6: the masquers danced about

Shylock's house and then left; the "grim figure" of Shylock then "crossed to his dwelling, raised his right hand, struck twice upon the door with the iron knocker, and stood like a statue, waiting--while a slow-descending curtain closed in one of the most expressive pictures that any stage has ever presented." Although Shakespeare lacked the curtain, no doubt he could have achieved a similar effect had he wished.

[2] The conventional locales for these scenes are: "a street" for scenes 2 and 4, "Shylock's house" for 3 (though there is no reason for the scene to be in-doors), and "before Shylock's house" for 5 and 6. The conventional locales date from the eighteenth century and have no textual authority. These scenes are generally performed with no attempt to shift the locale.

[3] Toby Lelyveld, Shylock on the Stage (Cleveland: P of Western Reserve U, 1960) 92.

Chapter VI

[1] "Shylock and Other Stage Jews," The Theatre, New Series 3 (1879): 198.

[2] See Chapter I, note 1.

[3] "The Original of Shylock," Gentleman's Magazine, February 1880: 196.

[4] Arthur Dimock, "The Conspiracy of Dr. Lopez," English Historical Review 9 (1894): 440-72 has a full account of Lopez's life with emphasis on his political activities. There is also a biography in The Dictionary of National Biography.

[5] E.g., J. D. Wilson 116-17; John Palmer, Comic Characters of Shakespeare (London: Macmillan, 1946) 53-55.

[6] Lee, "Original" 187; see also his "Jews in England before 1632," Academy 21 (1882): 194 and "Elizabethan England and the Jews," New Shakespere Society Transactions (1887-92) 143-66.

[7] "Jews in Elizabethan England," <u>Transactions of the Jewish Historical Society of England</u> 11 (1924-27) 1-91 (esp. 19).

[8] "A Colony of Jews in Shakespeare's London," <u>Essays and Studies</u> 23 (1937): 38-51 (esp. 51).

[9] <u>A History of the Jews in England</u>, 3rd ed. (Oxford: Oxford UP, 1964) 284.

[10] Cardozo 329. W. Smith, "Shakespeare's Shylock," <u>Shakespeare Quarterly</u> 15 (1964): 193-99.

[11] W. Smith 194.

[12] Gerald Friedlander, <u>Shakespeare and the Jew</u> (London: Routledge, 1921) 24-25; Myer Landa, <u>The Jew in Drama</u> (1926; New York: KTAV, 1969) 81; Hermann Sinsheimer, <u>Shylock: The History of a Character</u> (1947; New York: Citadel, 1964) 131.

[13] Sinsheimer 136.

[14] <u>Stratford to Dogberry: Studies in Shakespeare's Earlier Plays</u> (Pittsburgh: U of Pittsburgh P, 1961) 135.

[15] Arden xliii.

[16] <u>Politics</u>, tr. H. Rackham, Loeb ed. (1932) 51.

[17] Morris P. Tilley, <u>A Dictionary of the Proverbs in England in the Sixteenth and Seventeenth Centuries</u> (Ann Arbor: U of Michigan P, 1950) no. U28.

[18] Quoted from <u>The Geneva Bible: A Facsimile of the 1560 Edition</u>, ed. Lloyd E. Berry (Madison: U of Wisconsin P, 1969) 91.

[19] Benjamin N. Nelson, <u>The Idea of Usury</u>, 2nd ed. (Princeton: Princeton UP, 1969) has an excellent discussion of the history of the interpretation of Deut. 23.20, observing with wit that the Reformation transformed "Universal Brotherhood" into "Universal Otherhood."

164

[20] Ed. R. H. Tawney (New York: Harcourt Brace, [1925]) 284-85.

[21] Tawney's Introduction is 172 pages. The quotation is from p. 170.

[22] T. Wilson, ed. Tawney 177.

[23] "The Usurer in Elizabethan Drama," _PMLA_ 31 (1916): 190-91, 198.

[24] "Conventions" 192. See Chapter III, note 8.

[25] _Shakespeare in His Time and Ours_ (Notre Dame: U of Notre Dame P, 1968) 237-54. Also see Harold Fisch, "Shakespeare and the Puritan Dynamic," _Shakespeare Survey_ 27 (1964): 81-92.

[26] 5.1.97-99 in _The Plays of George Chapman, The Comedies_, ed. T. M. Parrott, 2 vols. (London: Routledge, 1914) 2: 658. The date of _Sir Giles Goosecap_ is 1606 according to the _OED_, but 1601-03 according to Alfred Harbage, _Annals of English Drama_, rev. S. Schoenbaum (Philadelphia: U of Pennsylvania P, 1964) 80.

[27] Quoted from _The Letters of Queen Elizabeth_, ed. G. B. Harrison (London, 1935) 22 by Dessen, "The Elizabethan Stage Jew and Christian Example: Gerontus, Barabas, and Shylock," _Modern Language Quarterly_ 35 (1974) 233.

[28] Hunter's "The Theology of Marlowe's _The Jew of Malta_" was first published in 1964, but is most readily available in _Christopher Marlowe's "The Jew of Malta": Text and Major Criticism_, ed. Irving Ribner (New York: Odyssey, 1970) 179-218; 186 cited. Marlowe is quoted from the text of the play in Ribner's edition.

[29] F. E. Hutchinson, ed., _The Works of George Herbert_ (Oxford: Oxford UP, 1941) 170-71.

[30] Hunter 185.

[31] The five instances not discussed are: <u>A Midsummer Night's Dream</u> 3.1.95, where Thisbe (speaking Pyramus' lines) calls herself a "most lovely Jew"; <u>Love's Labor's Lost</u> 3.1.135, where Costard with a curious suggestion of the pound-of-flesh story calls the diminutive Moth, "My sweet ounce of man's flesh, my incony [fine] Jew"; <u>Macbeth</u> 4.1.26, where the Witches add "Liver of blaspheming Jew" to their cauldron; and twice in the same sentence in <u>I Henry IV</u> 2.4.179, where Falstaff swears that the "sixteen" travelers were bound "or I am a Jew else, an Ebrew Jew."

[32] See Chapter I, note 5. Brown assigns the following to Compositor X: A1 (? the title page), C1-4^v (2.1.18-2.5.3), E1-4^v (2.9.29-3.2.102), G1-4^v (3.4.19-4.1.69), and I1-K2 (4.1.427 to the end). The rest is assigned to Y: A2 and A2^v together with signatures B, D, F, and H.

[33] Gollancz, <u>A Book of Homage to Shakespeare</u> (London: Oxford UP, 1916) 171-72; Kittredge, ed., <u>The Merchant of Venice</u> (Boston: Ginn, 1945) ix. A number of suggestions for the origin of <u>Shylock</u> are listed by Horace H. Furness, ed., <u>The Merchant of Venice</u>, New Variorum Shakespeare (Philadelphia: Lippincott, 1888) ix-x; J. R. Brown, Arden ed. 3; and Murray J. Levith, <u>What's in Shakespeare's Names</u> (New Haven: Shoe String, 1978) 81-82.

[34] Ed., <u>The Merchant of Venice</u>, New Penguin Shakespeare (London: Penguin Books, 1967) 171.

[35] Elze (Chapter IV, note 9) 282. The essay was first published in <u>Shakespeare Jahrbuch</u> for 1871.

[36] Cardozo (Chapter I, note 5) 219-23.

[37] The 1560 ed., ed. Berry (note 18, above). Shakespeare used the Geneva and Bishops Bibles: see Richmond Noble, <u>Shakespeare's Biblical Knowledge</u> (London: Society for Promoting Christian Knowledge, 1935) 58.

[38] Lea, <u>Italian Popular Comedy</u>, 2 vols. (London: Oxford UP, 1934) 2: 392. Moore, "Pantaloon as Shylock," <u>Boston Public Library Quarterly</u> 1 (1949): 33-42 (33 quoted).

[39] Moore 42.

[40] (Urbana: U of Illinois P, 1960) 224.

[41] A Study of Shakespeare (London, 1880) 151.

[42] "Marlowe and Shakespeare," Shakespeare Quarterly 15 (1964): 46.

Chapter VII

[1] Shakespeare as a Dramatic Artist, 3rd ed. (1893; New York: Dover Books, 1966) 61. The first edition appeared in 1885.

[2] Brown, Arden ed. 26. Joan O. Holmer, "'When Jacob Graz'd His Uncle Laban's Sheep': A New Source for The Merchant of Venice," Shakespeare Quarterly 36 (1985): 64-65 suggests Miles Mosse's The Arraignment and Conviction of Usurie (1595) as a source. Mosse refers to the story twice in passing, once to compare the treatment angry usurers were giving Mosse with the treatment Laban accorded Jacob and once to suggest that God will take the goods of usurers as He took Laban's and gave them "to holy Iacob." To say the least, Shakespeare's use is very different: Mosse suggests that usurers are like Laban, while Shylock parallels himself with Jacob.

[3] Arnold Williams, The Common Expositor: An Account of the Commentaries on Genesis, 1527-1633 (Chapel Hill: U of North Carolina P, 1948) 171. Williams cites Pererius, Peter Martyr, Rivetus, Calvin, Willet.

[4] Leah Woods Wilkins, "Shylock's Pound of Flesh and Laban's Sheep," Modern Language Notes 62 (1947): 29.

[5] For example, H. B. Charlton, Shakespearian Comedy (London: Methuen, 1938) 147-50 and John Hazel Smith, "Shylock: 'Devil Incarnation' or 'Poor Man . . . Wronged'?" Journal of English and Germanic Philology 60 (1961): 9-10.

6 "Shylock, Jacob, and God's Judgment," Shakespeare Quarterly 1 (1950): 255-59.

7 Kittredge 120.

8 "The Merchant of Venice" in Prefaces to Shakespeare, 2nd series (London: Sidgwick & Jackson, 1930): 98.

9 Charlton 151.

10 Palmer 79.

11 "Shylock and the 'Conditioned Imagination': A Reinterpretation," Shakespeare Quarterly 22 (1971): 11.

12 William Shakespeare: A Reader's Guide (New York: Noonday, 1963) 190.

13 Of course, Venice was not a city chartered by a central government; Shakespeare was thinking of an English town.

14 Lelyveld 31-32.

15 Nathaniel Holmes, "Shylock's Case," Western Galaxy 1 (1888): 209-17 was apparently the first to note the relevance of the courts of equity to The Merchant. The subject is discussed in detail by Maxine MacKay, "The Merchant of Venice: A Reflection of the Early Conflict Between Courts of Law and Courts of Equity," Shakespeare Quarterly 15 (1964): 371-75 and Mark E. Andrews, Law versus Equity in "The Merchant of Venice" (Boulder: U of Colorado P, 1965), written in 1935. See also W. Gordon Zeeveld, The Temper of Shakespeare's Thought (New Haven: Yale UP, 1974) 141ff. and W. Nicholas Knight, "Equity, The Merchant of Venice, and William Lambarde," Shakespeare Survey 27 (1974): 93-104.

16 Moulton 60-61.

Chapter VIII

[1] The Organization and Personnel of the Shakespearean Company (Princeton: Princeton UP, 1927) 246.

[2] John P. Collier, The History of English Dramatic Poetry to the Time of Shakespeare and Annals of the Stage to the Restoration, 3 vols. (London, 1879) 3: 299-302.

[3] Lelyveld 7.

[4] A critical edition of Granville's play appears in Christopher Spencer, Five Restoration Adaptations of Shakespeare (Urbana: U of Illinois P, 1965) 345-402.

[5] Roscius Anglicanus, ed. Montague Summers (London: Fortune, n.d.) 52.

[6] "Some Account of the Life &c. of Mr. William Shakespear," Works of Mr. William Shakespear, ed. Rowe, 7 vols. (London: Tonson, Curll, 1709-10) 1: xix-xx.

[7] "Granville's 'Stock-Jobbing Jew,'" Philological Quarterly 13 (1934): 12.

[8] Shakspeare's Dramatic Art, tr. L. Dora Schmitz, 2 vols. (London, 1914) 2: 126.

[9] William Shakespeare [tr. W. Archer et al.] (New York: Macmillan, 1924) 164.

[10] "Shylock," Journal of English and Germanic Philology 10 (1911) 236-79. See note 11 for the text quoted.

[11] "Shylock," Shakespeare Studies Historical and Comparative in Method, 2nd ed. (New York: Ungar, 1960) 269, 303, 320, 324-26, 328.

[12] The Art and Life of William Shakespeare (New York: Harcourt Brace, 1940) 245-46.

[13] _Shakespeare's Festive Comedy_ (Princeton: Princeton UP, 1959) 168, 179.

[14] Palmer 88.

[15] "The Jew in Western Drama," _Bulletin of the New York Public Library_ 72 (1968): 480.

[16] See note 6 above.

[17] "Remarks on the Plays of Shakespear" in Rowe's ed. 7: 321.

[18] Doran, _"Their Majesties' Servants": Annals of the English Stage from Thomas Betterton to Edmund Kean_, rev. R. W. Lowe, 3 vols. (London, 1888) 3: 69.

[19] Lelyveld 26.

[20] _The Dramatic Censor_, 2 vols. (London, 1770) 1: 287, 291.

[21] _Shakespeare and Elizabethan Poetry_ (London: Chatto and Windus, 1951) 171, 174.

[22] _Character and Characterization in Shakespeare_ (Detroit: Wayne State UP, 1962) 9, 31.

[23] Warren Smith 196, 198-99.

[24] Grebanier 90-93, 165.

[25] _Essays_ 564. T. O. has been identified as Richard Hole.

[26] _The British Critic_ 9 (1797) 362; _The Monthly Review_ 22 (1797) 9.

[27] From _Characters of Shakespear's Plays_ (1817) in _The Complete Works of William Hazlitt_, ed. P. P. Howe, 21 vols. (London: Dent, 1930-34) 4: 323-24.

[28] _Complete Works_ 4: 320.

[29] Winter 175.

[30] Winter 177-78, 195.

[31] A Study of "The Merchant of Venice" (London: 1927) 10-11.

[32] The Meaning of Shakespeare (Chicago: U of Chicago P, 1951) 100-01.

[33] English Comedy (New York: Macmillan, 1929) 107.

[34] Charlton 127-29, 153. The essay was first published in Bulletin of the John Rylands Library 18 (1934): 34-68.

[35] Shakespeare (London: Cape, 1936) 161, 163-64.

[36] An Interpretation of Shakespeare (New York: Dryden, 1948) 118.

[37] Endeavors of Art (Madison: U of Wisconsin P, 1954) 319.

[38] Notes on Shakespeare's Workmanship (New York: Holt, 1917) 89.

[39] Ariosto, Shakespeare, and Corneille, tr. Douglas Ainslie (New York: Holt, 1920) 217.

[40] "Shakespeare's Portrayal of Shylock," Essays in Dramatic Literature: The Parrott Presentation Volume, ed. Hardin Craig (Princeton: Princeton UP, 1935) 225, 238.

[41] Quoted from the later version in Brown's Shakespeare's Plays in Performance (London: Arnold, 1966) 81, 90. Published earlier in The Early Shakespeare, ed. J. R. Brown and Bernard Harris, Stratford-upon-Avon Studies 3 (London: Arnold, 1961) 186-209.

Selected Bibliography

This bibliography lists about one hundred books and articles that are especially useful for an historical and critical understanding of _The Merchant of Venice_. Many of the works are not cited in the notes, and some cited in the notes are not listed here (the references for the latter may be found through the author's name in the index). Several editions of the play are included for the sake of their valuable notes or introductions: see J. R. Brown, Furness, Greg, Merchant, Pooler, and J. D. Wilson. John Wilders' casebook cited below contains selections from many works listed individually, including those by Auden, Barber, Bradbrook, J. R. Brown (_Shakespeare and His Comedies_), Burckhardt, Freud, Goddard, Granville-Barker, Midgley, Moulton, Palmer, Plowman, and Stoll. Sylvan Barnet's _Twentieth Century Views_ has selections from works listed by Auden, Barber, J. R. Brown (_Shakespeare and His Comedies_), Granville-Barker, Kermode, Lewalski, and Moody. Two book-length bibliographies are included: Tannenbaum's covers works written through 1940, while Wheeler's, which is annotated, lists mostly works from 1940 to 1979.

Shakespeare Quarterly publishes a bibliography annually.

Andrews, Mark E. *Law versus Equity in "The Merchant of Venice."* Boulder: U of Colorado P, 1965.

Auden, W. H. *The Dyer's Hand and Other Essays.* New York: Random House, 1962.

Barber, C[esar] L. *Shakespeare's Festive Comedy.* Princeton: Princeton UP, 1959.

Barnet, Sylvan, ed. *Twentieth Century Interpretations of "The Merchant of Venice."* Englewood Cliffs: Prentice-Hall, 1970.

Baskervill, Charles R. "Bassanio as an Ideal Lover." *The Manly Anniversary Studies in Language and Literature.* Chicago: U of Chicago P, 1923. 90-103.

Bradbrook, M[uriel] C. *Shakespeare and Elizabethan Poetry.* London: Chatto and Windus, 1951.

Brown, Beatrice D. "Mediaeval Prototypes of Lorenzo and Jessica." *Modern Language Notes* 44 (1929): 227-32.

Brown, John R., ed. *The Merchant of Venice.* Arden Shakespeare. London: Methuen, 1955.

---. "The Realization of Shylock: A Theatrical Criticism." *Early Shakespeare.* Ed. J. R. Brown and B. Harris. Stratford-upon-Avon Studies 3. London: Arnold, 1961. 186-209. Pub. with alterations as "Creating a Role: Shylock" in Brown's *Shakespeare's Plays in Performance.* London: Arnold, 1966. 71-90.

---. *Shakespeare and His Comedies.* London: Methuen, 1957.

Bryant, Joseph A. <u>Hippolyta's View</u>. Lexington: U of Kentucky P, 1961.

Bullough, Geoffrey. <u>Narrative and Dramatic Sources of Shakespeare</u>. Vol. 1. London: Routledge and Kegan Paul; New York: Columbia UP, 1957. 8 vols. 1957-75.

Burckhardt, Sigurd. "<u>The Merchant of Venice</u>: The Gentle Bond." <u>ELH</u> 29 (1962): 239-62.

Cardozo, Jacob L. <u>The Contemporary Jew in the Elizabethan Drama</u>. Amsterdam, 1925. New York: Burt Franklin, n.d.

Charlton, H[enry] B. <u>Shakespearian Comedy</u>. London: Methuen, 1938.

Coe, Charles N. <u>Demi-Devils: The Character of Shakespeare's Villains</u>. New York: Bookman, 1963.

Coghill, Nevill. "The Basis of Shakespearian Comedy." <u>Essays and Studies</u> ns 3 (1950): 1-28.

Cohen, D[erek] M. "The Jew and Shylock." <u>Shakespeare Quarterly</u> 31 (1980): 53-63.

Colley, John S. "Launcelot, Jacob, and Esau: Old and New Law in <u>The Merchant of Venice</u>." <u>Yearbook of English Studies</u> 10 (1980): 181-89.

Danson, Lawrence. <u>The Harmonies of "The Merchant of Venice</u>." New Haven: Yale UP, 1978.

Dessen, Alan C. "The Elizabethan Stage Jew and Christian Example: Gerontus, Barabas, and Shylock." <u>Modern Language Quarterly</u> 35 (1974) 231-45.

Dimock, Arthur. "The Conspiracy of Dr. Lopez." <u>English Historical Review</u> 9 (1894): 440-72.

Draper, John W. <u>Stratford to Dogberry</u>. Pittsburgh: U of Pittsburgh P, 1961.

174

Echeruo, Michael J. C. "Shylock and the 'Conditioned Imagination': A Reinterpretation." <u>Shakespeare Quarterly</u> 22 (1971) 3-15.

Evans, Bertrand. <u>Shakespeare's Comedies</u>. London: Oxford UP, 1960.

Fieldler, Leslie A. <u>The Stranger in Shakespeare</u>. London: Croom Helm, 1973.

Fisch, Harold. "Shakespeare and the Puritan Dynamic." <u>Shakespeare Survey</u> 27 (1974): 81-92.

Freud, Sigmund. "The Theme of the Three Caskets." 1913. <u>The Standard Edition of the Complete Psychological Works of Sigmund Freud</u>. Tr. and ed. James Strachey et al. Vol. 12. London: Hogarth, 1963. 291-301. 23 vols. 1953-66.

Fujimura, Thomas H. "Mode and Structure in <u>The Merchant of Venice</u>." <u>PMLA</u> 81 (1966): 499-511.

Furness, Horace H., ed. <u>The Merchant of Venice</u>. New Variorum Edition. Philadelphia: Lippincott, 1888.

Goddard, Harold C. <u>The Meaning of Shakespeare</u>. Chicago: U of Chicago P, 1951.

Gollancz, Israel. <u>Allegory and Mysticism in Shakespeare: A Medievalist on "The Merchant of Venice</u>." London: Jones, 1931.

Graham, Cary B. "Standards of Value in <u>The Merchant of Venice</u>." <u>Shakespeare Quarterly</u> 4 (1953): 145-51.

Granville, George. <u>The Jew of Venice</u>. London, 1701. In <u>Five Restoration Adaptations of Shakespeare</u>. Ed. Christopher Spencer. Urbana: U of Illinois P, 1965.

Granville-Barker, Harley. <u>Prefaces to Shakespeare</u>. 2nd ser. London: Sidgwick & Jackson, 1930.

Grebanier, Bernard. <u>The Truth about Shylock</u>. New York: Random House, 1962.

Greg, W. W., ed. The Merchant of Venice: 1600 (Hayes Quarto). Shakespeare Quarto Facsimiles, no. 2. Oxford: Oxford UP, 1957.

Hapgood, Robert. "Portia and The Merchant of Venice: The Gentle Bond." Modern Language Quarterly 28 (1967): 19-32.

Harbage, Alfred. William Shakespeare: A Reader's Guide. New York: Noonday, 1963.

Hazlitt, William. Characters of Shakespear's Plays. London, 1817.

Holmer, Joan O. "The Education of the Merchant of Venice." Studies in English Literature 1500-1900 25 (1985): 307-35.

Holmes, Martin. Shakespeare's Public: The Touchstone of His Genius. London: Murray, 1960.

Hunter, G. K. "Elizabethans and Foreigners." Shakespeare Survey 17 (1964): 37-52.

Hurrell, John D. "Love and Friendship in The Merchant of Venice." Texas Studies in Literature and Language 3 (1961): 328-41.

Hyman, Lawrence W. "The Rival Lovers in The Merchant of Venice." Shakespeare Quarterly 21 (1970): 109-16.

Jameson, Anna B. Characteristics of Women, Moral, Poetical, and Historical. 1832. 2nd ed. London, 1833.

Jones, Eldred. "Racial Terms for Africans in Elizabethan Usage." Review of National Literatures 3.2 (1972): 54-89.

Jordan, William C. "Approaches to the Court Scene in the Bond Story: Equity and Mercy or Reason and Nature." Shakespeare Quarterly 33 (1982): 49-59.

Kermode, Frank. "The Mature Comedies." Early Shakespeare. Ed. J. R. Brown and B. Harris. Stratford-upon-Avon Studies 3. London: Arnold, 1961. 211-27.

Kirschbaum, Leo. Character and Characterization in Shakespeare. Detroit: Wayne State UP, 1962.

Knight, W. Nicholas. "Equity, The Merchant of Venice, and William Lambarde." Shakespeare Survey 27 (1974): 93-104.

Lee, Sidney L. "The Original of Shylock." Gentleman's Magazine. Feb. 1880: 185-200.

Lelyveld, Toby. Shylock on the Stage. Cleveland: P of Western Reserve U, 1960.

Lewalski, Barbara K. "Biblical Allusions and Allegory in The Merchant of Venice." Shakespeare Quarterly 13 (1962): 327-43.

Long, John H. Shakespeare's Use of Music: A Study of the Music and Its Performance in the Original Production of Seven Comedies. Gainesville: U of Florida P, 1955.

MacCary, W. Thomas. Friends and Lovers: The Phenomenology of Desire in Shakespearean Comedy. New York: Columbia UP, 1985.

MacKay, Maxine. "The Merchant of Venice: A Reflection of the Early Conflict Between Courts of Law and Courts of Equity." Shakespeare Quarterly 15 (1964): 371-75.

Merchant, W. Moelwyn, ed. The Merchant of Venice. New Penguin Shakespeare. Harmondsworth: Penguin, 1967.

Midgley, Graham. "The Merchant of Venice: A Reconsideration." Essays in Criticism 10 (1960): 119-33.

Moody, A[nthony] D. Shakespeare: "The Merchant of
     Venice." London: Arnold, 1964.

Moulton, Richard G. Shakespeare as a Dramatic Artist.
     3rd ed. 1893. New York: Dover, 1965.

Muir, Kenneth.   Shakespeare's Comic Sequence.
     Liverpool: Liverpool UP, 1979.

---. The Sources of Shakespeare's Plays. London:
     Methuen, 1977.

Murry, John Middleton. Shakespeare. London: Cape,
     1936.

Nelson, Benjamin N. The Idea of Usury. 2nd ed.
     Princeton: Princeton UP, 1969.

O., T. [Richard Hole?] "An Apology for the Character
     and Conduct of Shylock." In Essays by a Society
     of Gentlemen, at Exeter. No editor. London,
     [1796]. 552-73.

Palmer, John. Comic Characters of Shakespeare.
     London: Macmillan, 1946.

Pettet, E. C. "The Merchant of Venice and the Problem
     of Usury." Essays and Studies 31 (1945): 19-33.

Pettigrew, Helen P. "Bassanio, the Elizabethan Lover."
     Philological Quarterly 16 (1937): 296-306.

Phialas, Peter G. Shakespeare's Romantic Comedies.
     Chapel Hill: U of North Carolina P, 1966.

Plowman, Max. "Money and The Merchant." The Right to
     Live. London, 1942. 177-82.

Pooler, Charles K., ed. The Merchant of Venice. Arden
     Edition. 1905. 4th ed. London: Methuen, 1917.

Rosenberg, Edgar. From Shylock to Svengali: Jewish
     Stereotypes in English Fiction. Stanford:
     Stanford UP, 1960.

---. "The Jew in Western Drama." <u>Bulletin of the New York Public Library</u> 72 (1968): 442-91. Reprinted in Edward D. Coleman. <u>The Jew in English Drama: An Annotated Bibliography</u>. New York Public Library and KTAV, 1970.

Roth, Cecil. "The Background of Shylock." <u>Review of English Studies</u> 9 (1933): 148-56.

---. <u>A History of the Jews in England</u>. 1941. 3rd ed. London: Oxford UP, 1964.

Salingar, Leo. <u>Shakespeare and the Traditions of Comedy</u>. Cambridge: Cambridge UP, 1974.

Schlauch, Margaret. "The Pound of Flesh Story in the North." <u>Journal of English and Germanic Philology</u> 30 (1931): 348-60.

Siegel, Paul N. <u>Shakespeare in His Time and Ours</u>. Notre Dame: U of Notre Dame P, 1968.

Sinsheimer, Hermann. <u>Shylock: The History of a Character</u>. 1947. New York: Citadel, 1964.

Sisson, C[harles] J. "A Colony of Jews in Shakespeare's London." <u>Essays and Studies</u> 23 (1937): 38-51.

Smith, John Hazel. "Shylock: 'Devil Incarnation' or 'Poor Man . . . Wronged'?" <u>Journal of English and Germanic Philology</u> 60 (1961): 1-21.

Smith, Warren D. "Shakespeare's Shylock." <u>Shakespeare Quarterly</u> 15 (1964): 193-99.

Spencer, Christopher. "Shakespeare's <u>Merchant of Venice</u> in Sixty-Three Editions." <u>Studies in Bibliography</u> 25 (1972): 89-106.

Stoll, Elmer Edgar. "Shylock." <u>Shakespeare Studies Historical and Comparative in Method</u>. 2nd ed. New York: Ungar, 1960. 255-336. First pub. in <u>Journal of English and Germanic Philology</u> 10 (1911): 236-79.

Stonex, Arthur B. "The Usurer in Elizabethan Drama." PMLA 31 (1916): 190-210.

Tannenbaum, Samuel A. Shakspere's "The Merchant of Venice" (A Concise Bibliography). New York: the author, 1941.

Van Doren, Mark. Shakespeare. New York: Holt, 1939.

Walley, Harold R. "Shakespeare's Portrayal of Shylock." Essays in Dramatic Literature: The Parrott Presentation Volume. Ed. Hardin Craig. Princeton: Princeton UP, 1935. 213-42.

Wilders, John, ed. Shakespeare: "The Merchant of Venice": A Casebook. London: Macmillan, 1969.

Wilkins, Leah Woods. "Shylock's Pound of Flesh and Laban's Sheep." Modern Language Notes 62 (1947): 28-30.

Wilson, John Dover, ed. The Merchant of Venice. The New Shakespeare. Cambridge: Cambridge UP, 1926.

---. Shakespeare's Happy Comedies. London: Faber & Faber, 1962.

Wilson, J[ohn] Harold. "Granville's 'Stock-Jobbing Jew.'" Philological Quarterly 13 (1934): 1-15.

Winter, William. Shakespeare on the Stage. New York: Moffat, Yard, 1911.

Wright, Celeste Turner. "Some Conventions Regarding the Usurer in Elizabethan Literature." Studies in Philology 31 (1934): 176-97.

---. "The Usurer's Sin in Elizabethan Literature." Studies in Philology 35 (1938): 178-94.

Zeeveld, W. Gordon. The Temper of Shakespeare's Thought. New Haven: Yale UP, 1974.

Index

STUDIES IN BRITISH LITERATURE